TWAYNE'S WORLD AUTHORS SERIES
A Survey of the World's Literature

SPAIN

Janet W. Díaz, University of North Carolina at Chapel Hill
EDITOR

Alonso de Castillo Solórzano

TWAS 457

Madrid, with the River Manzanares in the
Foreground

ALONSO DE CASTILLO SOLÓRZANO

By ALAN SOONS

State University of
New York at Buffalo

TWAYNE PUBLISHERS
A DIVISION OF G. K. HALL & CO., BOSTON

Library of Congress Cataloging in Publication Data

Soons, Alan.
    Alonso de Castillo Sólorzano.

    (Twayne's world authors series ; TWAS 457 :
Spain)
    Bibliography: p. 135–141
    1. Castillo Sólorzano, Alonso de, 1584–1647?—
Criticism and interpretation.
PQ6321.C55Z88   863'.3   78-39
ISBN 0-8057-6294-9

Contents

About the Author

Alan Soons was born in Grantham, England, in 1925 and educated at the universities of Sheffield and Nottingham (England), Zaragoza (Spain) and at Harvard. He has been a member of the faculty of the universities of St. Andrews (Scotland), the West Indies, Mona (Jamaica), Massachusetts at Amherst, and Rice, before joining that of the State University of New York at Buffalo in 1972. He is author of *Ficción y comedia en el Siglo de Oro* (Madrid, 1967) and *Haz y envés del cuento risible en el Siglo de Oro* (London, 1976), besides numerous articles and review-articles dealing with fictional and dramatic works of the Spanish Golden Age.

Preface

In this book it is hoped that the reader will become acquainted with a Spanish author who was above everything else a producer in abundance of works of entertainment. These took the form of short romances or novellas, longer works of fiction, some three-act plays, interludes (that is, *entremeses*, examples of a uniquely Spanish type of playlet) and jocular poems. After a sympathetic reading of his work, Castillo Solórzano may easily make his impression on us of being a writer of very diffuse talents and one unconcerned with the great issues of his time, when compared with illustrious men among his immediate predecessors. We may miss perhaps that urgency perceptible in the justly celebrated fictions of Mateo Alemán, Miguel de Cervantes and Lope de Vega. Yet Castillo Solórzano has his own, smaller, excellences, and this book will have achieved its objective if it has guided the reader in their direction and, moreover, if it has situated an entertaining figure among authors within a continuing European literary tradition.

Considerations of space have brought with them the necessity for limiting the discussion of Castillo's production in detail. The fifty-four short novellas will, therefore, be treated largely as a single phenomenon for a collective type of analysis. The contributions which Castillo made to the literature of roguery in his century certainly must claim the greater part of our attention, since in these works he blundered into the question of woman's place in a masculine society of criminals and confidence-tricksters.

Our author has been neglected, by and large, in his capacity of dramatist; it is hoped that the chapters devoted to his five interludes and seven plays will illuminate the essentials of his thought and artistic practice. These essentials are displayed equally in both dramatic form and the spate of short novellas Castillo devoted to the loves and adventures of idealized young people.

The concluding portion of this book is intended as a contribution towards estimating the prodigious effect which Castillo Solórzano's works in all genres have exerted on the literatures of various foreign countries. One is tempted to speculate that it was he more than any other writer who stimulated, quite unwittingly, the production of all those fictional forms we loosely call nowadays "romances": all those literary and sub-literary appeals to our yearning for the fulfillment of our wishes, in some ever-receding never-never-land of the "life of action" and the "life of love." Though perhaps not single-handedly, Castillo Solórzano had much to do also with the elaboration of a type of fictional character who was to find fortune in the works of coming centuries: the humorist.

Also included, to show his lyrical and satirical talents, are twenty or so poetic pieces by Castillo from his contribution to the published offering of a literary society, the exceedingly rare book *Parnassus Jesting (Donaires del Parnaso,* 1624). An attempt has been made to render these pieces into appropriate English prose.

An expression of gratitude must be made here for the help extended by many librarians, at the Biblioteca Nacional, Madrid, the Boston Public Library, and university libraries at Harvard, the University of Massachusetts and the State University of New York at Buffalo. Very special thanks are due to the Julian Park Fund trustees at the State University of New York at Buffalo for generous monetary help in preparing this work.

ALAN SOONS

State University of
New York at Buffalo

Chronology

1584 Alonso de (sometimes alternating with "del" on page-head-ings within a single work) Castillo Solórzano, son of Francisco de(l) Castillo and Ana Griján, born at Tordesillas, northern Spain.

1597 Death of the elder Castillo, a steward in the household of the Dukes of Alba.

1616 Alonso suffers a near-fatal illness in January. Death of his mother. Referred to as married (to Augustina de Paz).

1618 Financial difficulties and further grave sickness afflict Alonso. He moves to Madrid, and is said to have adopted a daughter (Ana de Velarde). He is secretary of a literary society, the Academia Mantuana ("Mantua" being a learned name for Madrid), directed by Sebastián Francisco de Medrano.

1619 Alonso's first printed poem, among the preliminaries of Cris-tóbal González de Torneo's *Vida y penitencia de Santa Teo-dora (Life and Penitence of St. Theodora)*.

1620 Enters the service of the Count of Benavente.

1621 Contributes to a contest of poems in honor of St. Isidro, but forfeits the third prize because he had used a pseudonym.

1622 Reportedly in service to the Marquis of Villar.

1623 Obliged to sell his own title of nobility and lands he held in Tordesillas.

1624 First publication, *Donaires del Parnaso (Parnassus Jesting)*, a collection of his own and others' verses.

1625 First collection of novellas, *Tardes entretenidas (Evening Entertainments)*.

1626 Publishes *Jornadas alegres (Merry Days)*.

1627 *Tiempo de regocijo (Time of Rejoicing)*, a miscellany includ-ing his interlude *El casamentero (The Marriage-Broker)*.

1628 Moves to Valencia as *major-domo* of the Marquis of Los Vélez. Publishes his first long fictional work, *Escarmientos de amor (Love's Chastenings)*.

1629 Rewrites *Escarmientos* as *Lisardo enamorado (Lisardo in Love)*, and publishes a novella-collection, *Huerta de Valencia*

(Plain of Valencia), containing his first three-act drama *El agravio satisfecho (Outrage Atoned For)*.

1631   Said to take up residence in Barcelona. Publishes the collection *Noches de placer (Nights of Pleasure)*, and an episodic novel concerning *pícaras*, *Las harpías en Madrid (The Harpies in Madrid)*, also containing his interlude *El comisario de figuras (The Censor of Eccentrics)*.

1632   Another episodic tale of a *pícara*, *La niña de los embustes (The Female Scoundrel)* containing two interludes—*El barbador (The Beard-Maker)* and *La prueba de los doctores (The Test of the Physicians)*.

1633   Publishes a long composite fiction, *Los amantes andaluces (The Andalusian Lovers)*.

1634   Victory of the Imperial (including Spanish), forces at Nördlingen in Germany, celebrated by Castillo in an unpublished play *La victoria de Norlingen*. Publishes a novella-collection, *Fiestas del jardín (Garden Festivals)* containing three comedies, *Los encantos de Bretaña (Enchantments in Brittany))*, *La fantasma de Valencia (The Specter of Valencia)*, and *El marqués del Cigarral (The Marquis from the Toledo Suburbs)*.

1635   Moves to Zaragoza. Publishes *Sagrario de Valencia (Sacristy of Valencia)*, an "Account of . . . objects of devotion in Valencia."

1636   Publishes the devotional treatise *Patrón de Alcira (St. Bernard, Patron Saint of Alcira)*, and probably writes his only religious drama, in one act, *The Fire Sent from Heaven (El fuego dado del cielo)*.

1637   Publishes the episodic novel of the adventures of a scoundrel *Aventuras del bachiller Trapaza (Adventures of Quick-Talking Trapaza)*. It includes his interlude *La castañera (The Chestnut-Vendor)*.

1639   *El mayorazgo figura (The Lordly Buffoon)* produced on the Madrid stage. Publishes two more popular biographies, *Historia de Marco Antonio y Cleopatra (The Story of Mark Antony and Cleopatra)* and *Epítome de la vida y hechos del Rey Don Pedro de Aragón (Summary of the Life and Deeds of King Peter III of Aragon)*.

1640   Publishes a novella-collection *Los alivios de Casandra (To Cheer up Casandra)* including the play *El mayorazgo figura*, and also the miscellany *Sala de recreación (The Salon)*, which includes the play *La torre de Florisbella (Florisbella's Tower)*.

1642   Publishes another episodic novel, of a female scoundrel, *La garduña de Sevilla y anzuelo de las bolsas (The She-Stoat of Seville, Fishhook of the Purses of Others)*.

1643   Castillo may have accompanied the Marquis of Los Vélez, whose secretary he was, on his embassy to Rome (1641), or to Sicily where he was Viceroy (1643–1647).

1648   Castillo known to be no longer living.

1649   Posthumous publication of the last collection of novellas under Castillo's name: *La quinta de Laura (Laura's Country House)*.

1667   Publication of *La victoria de Norlingen* in Part 28 of an anthology of dramas, *Comedias nuevas*.

CHAPTER 1

The Life and Times of
Castillo Solórzano

A LONSO de Castillo Solórzano came to manhood at the end of
the reign of Philip II, the Prudent King. The kingdom, and
especially its gaunt heartland of Castile, was by then showing
economic and social strain after many generations of warfare and
ill-directed administration, aimed at containment of Protestants,
Turks and internal rebels, and advancement of the fortunes of the
House of Austria. Philip's kingdom, too, had the unhappy lot of
experiencing ahead of the other states of Europe the effects of a
monetary inflation, caused mainly by the influx of the silver coming
from Spain's own American territories into a Europe which produced too few things to buy with it.

The king had never relaxed his warlike policy, so that what wealth
could be taxed—and by a fiscal anomaly this was chiefly that wealth
held by the landowners and traders of Castile—produced revenues
to be spent on armies, fortresses and fleets. Many Castilian
landowners, therefore, were quite willing to sell out, acquire an-
nuities of doubtful rentability from the government and move into
the cities. We shall observe some of Castillo's characters doing this,
and also their creator.

A worse disaster than the death of the aged king was to befall
Spain in the last years of the century. This was the great plague and
its attendant famine, which brought to nothing the economic plans,
precarious at best, evolved in the old king's reign. The economy and
the social order of Spain never really recovered from this misfortune
during the whole of the seventeenth century. It is always hazardous
to relate the mentality of a nation and an epoch to particular disas-
ters, but the hypothesis is worth putting forward that the appetite of
literate Spaniards for totally frivolous comedies, novels and mere

13

word-games may have been determined by a deep desire for distraction from this accumulation of ills. A large section of society apparently sought to be amused at all costs; Castillo Solórzano helped to amuse it.

Madrid, Castillo's home in middle life, and the object of nostalgia for him later, underwent a great transformation under the new king Philip III. The capital's population doubled in the one generation which that reign spanned, but the new *madrileños* tended to be marginal; in Castillo's nautical phraseology they (and he) were "skiffs," not "galleons," blown about on the ocean of Philip's capital. These individuals must have resembled the *colegio buscón* (college of sharpers) in Francisco de Quevedo's *Life of Pablos the Sharper* (*La vida del buscón Pablos,* 1626, but written much earlier), but such starving vagabonds must have impressed him, if his works are any indication, far less than the real-life Don Rodrigo Calderón y Sandelín. Here was a true "Proteus of Madrid," who through his impostures acquired celebrity and high offices in the army and the state during the government of his protector, the Duke of Lerma. It all ended with Lerma's demotion, and Calderón had a final brief day of celebrity on the scaffold. Not impoverished *pícaros* (delinquent rogues) but perhaps rather impudent social climbers with a capacity for relentless duping of their fellows would then be to the taste of the reading public.

The story of Spain during the rest of Castillo's life is that of the energy and resilience of the royal minister the Count-Duke of Olivares. Like poor Don Bernardo and his daughter in Castillo's *Outrage Atoned For* (*El agravio satisfecho,* 1629) Spain herself turned out to have an Andalusian aristocrat who would relieve her suffering. But there were, unfortunately, ancient structures and enmities within Spain which precluded the carrying out of the projects he initiated. Portugal and the Catalans revolted in 1640; Castillo was probably dead by the time (1648) that Naples rose in revolt also.

It is time to situate the obscure life of Castillo Solórzano in this particular epoch of Spanish history. Extremely little, however, is known with certainty about the life of the author beyond that he was a native of the small rural town of Tordesillas in the present-day province of Valladolid, which in its turn forms part of the ancient kingdom of Old Castile. We learn that his father, Francisco de Castillo, was a steward—or at least a rural representative—of the powerful Duke of Alba. Of the antecedents of his mother Ana de Griján we know absolutely nothing. Castillo's youth and early manhood cannot surely have been all misfortunes, but the surviving documents are as it happens concentrated on these: his father's death in 1597 and the circumstances of an implacable approach of penury. We know nothing of the personality of Agustina de Paz who was to be his wife, or even of the date, perhaps close to that of Castillo's thirtieth year, of their marriage. It is possible that she died not long afterwards, since there is a vague account of Castillo's adoption of a daughter, Ana de Velarde, possibly as an insurance against his old age. Indeed, it would be accurate to say that from about 1618, the date of Castillo's taking up residence in Madrid, his story is that of his books and of his activities as organizing secretary of at least one notable literary society in the capital. It seems that he was, from 1628 onwards, rarely if ever in Madrid, and we must suppose that he occupied himself in concealing feelings of frustration in his provincial exile from his noble master, the Marquis of Los Vélez. The date and the circumstances of his death are undiscoverable; we do learn that he was no longer alive in 1648.

Three areas of general information extant about Castillo may be useful for our understanding of him. First there is his family origin in the progressively impoverished class of the minor gentry of Old Castile, those whose little wealth had been derived since the Middle Ages from holding small parcels of land. From a meticulous recent study of Valladolid and its region at the end of the sixteenth century[1] we learn that the population of Tordesillas, Castillo's native town, had declined disastrously precisely between 1561 and 1591, and that families such as his were turning away from agriculture towards monetary speculation and, eventually, parasitism on more substantial groups in society.[2] We observe also, from the same study, that the region as a whole never recovered from the shift of Spain's royal and administrative capital back from Valladolid to Madrid in 1606. The extent and the effects of occurrences such as the plagues already referred to, and the attendant movements of popular unrest in the last years of the century may eventually be better documented. The region of Tordesillas was certainly among those worst affected. Prosperity at this moment in Spanish history had transposed itself to the south of Spain, close to the ports trading with the Americas—we shall see later that one of Castillo's dramatic characters, Don Bernardo in *Outrage Atoned For (El agravio satis-fecho,* 1629) moves from penurious Aragon southwards to Seville in the hope of avoiding ruin—but Castillo never seems to have visited the South himself. Ironically, the groups who had fed on the ruin of Castillo's kind sat in his audience or read his books. These were the landed magnates, whose presumed system of values Castillo adu-lates incessantly, and the city mercantilist group who offered the mortgages and the *cédulas* (promises of payment) into which the minor gentry converted its holdings.

Secondly, Castillo depended, for his perennially precarious liv-ing, on posts in the households of certain noblemen: the Count of Benavente, the Marquis of Villar and possibly others. Due to the fact that these men were from time to time royal representatives outside of Castile, our author frequently lived in outlying provincial cities when he might have wished personally to remain close to Madrid literary circles. On the other hand, he seems to have been able rapidly to secure a new local public for his writings, notably in Valencia and Saragossa, even though this entailed producing deriva-tive hackwork of purely provincial or devotional interest.

Finally, those meager biographical accounts surviving on Castillo situate him as a man of importance, when not an involuntary expa-triate, in the little world of the *academias* or literary societies. In his capacities of participant and secretary of an influential *academia* in Madrid, the one promoted by Sebastián Francisco de Medrano be-tween 1617 and 1622,[3] he acquired knowledge of what popular taste beyond that immediate coterie would demand in the way of literary fare: texts in verse, prose or dramatic form, filled with a rather predictable, relentless persiflage and facetiousness. It is undoubt-edly to this realization on Castillo's part that we owe his authorship of *entremeses,* or one-act "parades," the most memorable scenes—that is, the funny ones—in his three-act plays, and the element of impishness and *grotesquerie* which redeems what historians have usually called his "picaresque novels," better named "novels of swindling." The novellas[4] of love and fortune, which Castillo put forth in a parallel stream to these last stories of female cheats and their companions, apparently owe their existence, with their identifiably "dramatic" plots,[5] to the peculiarly exclusive state of the theaters in those decades; the public had its favorites among play-wrights and Castillo, for all his elite connections in the *academias,* was not one of them.[6] What we should today call the power of the box-office was, for unusual historical reasons, paramount in Spain and tended to give special prestige to Lope de Vega. However, Castillo, rueful though he says he is about the blocking of his career as playwright, seems not to think ill of the successful Lope. His references to him, on the contrary, are always full of praise. The two men of letters stood, after all, on different wings of the same literary movement supporting the monarchical and aristocratic dispensation in a perplexing time of governmental and economic crisis.[7] Lope in serious works and Castillo in trivial and ludicrous ones both help to reinforce a mythology of aristocracy and ancient virtue, probably without being conscious of doing so.

We have very little to work on to arrive at an idea of Castillo as a person. Some of his contemporaries imply that he was physically rather ugly: prematurely bald, with dark eyes and a wide mouth with few teeth. On the other hand, he dressed neatly, as would be most proper for one serving the nobility. His pleasant disposition seems to have charmed not a few people. We learn also that he was inclined at all times to praise fellow writers, never detracting from anyone's work if it showed true originality—we must not identify the merciless critics among his invented characters with their author. Certainly we have no mention of anyone speaking anything but good of him.

CHAPTER 2

Castillo's Interludes or Parades

THE principal concern of Castillo as a writer was to entertain his contemporaries, no matter how much he may have claimed to have had a moralizing intention. At the outset of any study of him, emphasis must fall on his capacity for being funny. This redeems much of the unevenness of his literary production.[1] A good area with which to begin a survey may therefore be his *entremeses* (interludes or "parades").

The origins of the kind of interlude written by Castillo are as yet unknown. Something comparable makes its appearance in France, Italy and England towards the end of the sixteenth century, in both dramatic and narrative form.[2] Perhaps it is a matter for the historian of social psychology: it could well be a symptom of a hardening of opinion in areas of public morality and class proprieties, among social groups who were in the seventeenth century to be assiduous applauders of the interlude. It is outside Spain, in Naples, that we first encounter the production of one of these "parades," *Master Palomo, Examiner* (1617), by the court dramatist Antonio Hurtado de Mendoza.[3] The characters represented in this work are mere hollow figures, each animated by some caprice or obsession, who appear in sequence before their examiner or censor. There is no anecdote or plot as such and true criticism of social behavior yields to plays on words and rapid jesting. No conduct is shown which might be imitated; this is merely a collection of figures somehow apart from the norm in society. Already we have the formula to be used by Castillo, as well as a sample of the kind of hollow, obsessed being presented in other works besides his interludes.

It is hard to establish dates for the writing or production of these pieces, surviving as part of Castillo's miscellaneous collections. The earliest is *The Marriage-Broker* (*El casamentero*, 1627). Here Piruétano first explains that he has a commission from the Papal

Nuncio of Toledo to sort out those who are going insane. His friend
Lázaro is, therefore, surprised to hear him proclaim himself to be a
marriage-broker instead. Three seekers of spouses appear: a projector, a poet and a woman. The first seeker reveals his latest plan: a
causeway to connect Spain with the Indies. After all, he says, the
council has approved his pilot-project, to connect Valencia with the
island of Ibiza, though it ran out of money before it could get
started. Piruétano has him overpowered, as being a madman.

Next the poet, speaking a *culto* (highly ornate and disjointed)
language, explains his dramatic activities and gives out some burlesque titles of plays. Piruétano and Lázaro listen to him, until he
imprudently insults the great Lope de Vega (who had just died in
1626) and is locked up forthwith. The poet is followed by the
woman, speaking a jargon comparable to that of Molière's *précieuses
ridicules* much later in the century: she explains that she would
dearly love to have a poet for a husband. However, when the poet
returns to the scene she exacts a promise that she must be allowed
to censor the plays he writes: ". . . *que no libraré faltas de su ingenio / en diversas tramoyas y exquisitas, . . .*" ("For I won't excuse
his lapses of invention in spite of varied and exquisite stage-machinery . . .") Here we are obliged to reflect on Castillo's own dramas,
which so often depend abjectly on the prodigal use of stage-
mechanisms! Her poet ruefully agrees to this, and the interlude
ends in a round-dance, each now proven madman wearing his or her
bonnet or "madcap."

The Marriage Broker is quite patently an imitation of *The Re-
pairer of Nature's Faults (El remendón de la naturaleza)*, an interlude by Alonso Jerónimo de Salas Barbadillo, Castillo's colleague
among the impoverished men of letters on the margin of Madrid's
society.[4] Salas's interlude was printed in 1622, and accompanying it
was a similar piece, *The Censor of Bad Taste (El comisario contra
malos gustos)*, upon which Castillo modeled his own *Censor of Eccentrics (El comisario de figuras*, 1631). The invention is relatively
weak in this interlude, in which Castillo introduces a similar com-
missioner from the nuncio to announce his hope of being useful in
clearing Madrid of eccentrics. The first usher *(alguacil)* escorts a
beribboned man-about-town, who is forthwith sentenced to exchange his fancy hat, much adorned with ladies' favors, for the
madcap. This procedure of examination continues to the end of the
play where: there is a lady so presumptuous as to be able to fall in

love only with herself; a poet who helps himself to the work of others so that he may compete in literary contests (again, something of which Castillo had excellent knowledge); a nobleman who considers his claim to a good pedigree absolutely immaculate and unique; and a *culto* versifier caught in the act of perpetrating an unintelligible sonnet. The censor tires of sentencing them and of even looking at eccentrics. Once again the interlude ends in a dance, or rout.

A parade-type playlet which uncovers Castillo's special talents a little more happily is *The Beardmaker* (*El barbador*, 1632). Here Pescaño enters to announce that his accomplice Piruétano will undertake to make hair and beards grow on those who have none. Pescaño is diffident, fearing the worst will come of the project. The "patients" begin to appear while Piruétano makes unintelligible utterances for Pescaño to "interpret," and for them to overhear. The core of the piece is a farcical explanation by one of the bare-faces (*lampiños*) of how he came to be in his sorry state:

Preñada de mí, a mi madre	When she was pregnant with
diole un mal de madre un viernes,	me, one Friday my mother
de comerse un melón de agua,	began to suffer from a pain
que quiso todo comerle.	in the belly, from having
Dos médicos, no muy doctos,	attempted to eat a watermelon
la recetan que la echen,	whole. Two physicians, not
para aplacarsele el mal,	very learned ones, prescribed
una ayuda de agua fuerte.	for her a hot water enema.
Recibiola, y yo que estaba	She underwent this and I,
descuidado y en su vientre,	who was an innocent bystander
recibí el escopetazo	in her belly, received the salvo
del jeringal pistolete.	from the syringe. As it was the
Como era el séptimo mes	seventh month of her pregnancy
de su preñado, le vienen	the pains came upon her at once
al instante los dolores	and I was born that very Friday
y nací en el mismo viernes	with a scalded face. I got well
con la barba desollada.	again quite soon, and when I was
Sané della en tiempo breve,	baptized my godfather, to
y al darme el bautismo santo,	prevent my being chilled by the
porque helarme no pudiese	water, ordered it to be mixed
el agua, mandó el padrino	with warm water. They threw
mezclarla con más caliente.	boiling water into the font;
Echose hirviendo en la pila;	Doctor Lesmes dipped me in and
chapuzome el doctor Lesmes,	scalded his hands while I was
abrasándose las manos,	once more left without hair

y yo de nuevo peleme.
Esta es la causa, señor,
de que mi barba remede
a un guijarro de Torote.

on me. This, sir, is why my
chin resembles a pebble from
the brook of Torote.

(N B A E, p. 314)

For no particular reason this figure also claims to be a man of letters, a *culto* poet. But soon the arrival of dancing-partners is announced, and as the "patients" come to realize that they have been tricked, gaining only painted "beards" for their pains, Piruétano and Pescaño dance impudently off the stage.

The Test of the Physicians (La prueba de los doctores, 1632) is another of these little works, the subject matter of which very possibly went directly on to fortune later in the century in the "medical" scenes of the comedies of Molière. Here Ginés informs his friend Truchado that he has decided to put his wife Brígida's devotion to the test by feigning a serious illness. Three doctors eventually appear, Ribete, Rebenque and Matanga, to all of whom Ginés describes a pain he has suffered ever since an ape broke his wine bottle. This is a signal for the physicians to lapse into unintelligible medical jargon, with much ludicrous confusion of Latin authors' names, and to examine Ginés's urine (which is really a flask of wine). Brígida, impressed, confesses candidly that she hopes Ginés will not recover at all. The doctors adjourn—to talk about mules rather than patients, and to agree only in speaking ill of their absent colleague Dr. Mortaja—while Ginés comments sarcastically from his part of the stage. When they return to prescribe a remedy, Ginés alarms them by drinking the "urine." The doctors' shame is dissolved in a final dance.[5]

Rather later in date is *The Chestnut-Vendor (La castañera,* 1637), in the first scene of which Juana explains to Lucía how she was able to give up her old trade of selling roasted chestnuts in the street when she married a merchant of Seville. We learn that this husband has since gone to the Indies and died there, while she herself has moved to Madrid as a rich widow with many suitors. Four of these suitors now appear onstage: an apothecary, a tailor, a cobbler and a groom, all wishing to hide the identity of their trades. By innuendoes Juana infers of each one, to his mortification, what he really is in metaphors drawn from the vocabulary of each respective trade and its tools. The groom, however, is of tougher fiber and replies using a language which implies braziers and toasting. Now it is Juana's turn to feel chagrin. She accepts the groom, and there is the usual final dance.

What is the peculiar comic force which informs these interludes? And what was the ethical teaching supposedly passed on to audiences watching them? The answers to these questions are none too easy to formulate, though a beginning could be made by conceding that everyone in the audience must inevitably have felt a certain superiority to the absurd characters, while at the same time building up a vague sympathy with some of them as victims of "the way of the world" or human fragility. But this sympathy is not allowed to evolve by Castillo, since it cannot survive his immersion of character and situation in the ridiculous.[6] So we must expect no sustained warning against the activities of confidence men *(The Beard-Maker)* or of social pretenders *(The Chestnut-Vendor)*, but in its place merely a generalized impassivity on the dramatist's part before the imperfections of men and women who seem unaware—in contrast to the spectators who are presumably quite aware—of the essentials of normal living. It is all very close, therefore, to the art of farce, which depends on just such a tyranny of those loyal to "normal" values in everyday living, and who are consequently cruelly insensitive to others who someone has told them are deviant. This dramatic presentation does not imply the latent order beneath the confusions of the moment onstage as comedy does, but seems rather to be an intimation to the spectator of the basic instinctual anarchy which could be found if one were to search beneath the cruel imposition of society's conventions.

CHAPTER 3

Longer Dramatic Works of Castillo Solórzano

THE classic Spanish three-act drama was the result of many decades of experiment in the later sixteenth century. This slow
development was, however, interrupted by the astonishing individual activity of Lope de Vega in the last ten years of the century,
and it is impossible to speculate on how the Spanish dramatic forms
appearing in the wake of the labors of such men as Lope de Rueda,
Juan de la Cueva and Miguel de Cervantes would have evolved.
Lope de Vega notoriously stamped upon the three-act play, serious
and trivial, comic and tragic, a particularity it was never to lose until
well into the eighteenth century.[1] The playwrights after Lope
changed only superficial characteristics, never the underlying pattern.[2]

It is above all this notion of durable pattern which allows us to
speak of all Spanish three-act plays of the time as *comedias*, even
though they may have little of the traditionally comic in them,
without feeling the term to be an imprecise one. Formally, the
comedia possesses three acts and is always in verse with a notable
variation in metrical patterning from scene to scene. The meters
frequently adapt themselves in purely conventional manner according to the social status of the characters speaking the lines
(Italianate lyric meters in the mouths of characters "of quality";
more venerably "native" lyric meters in those of ancillary or nonserious characters). Meter also varies according to the mode in
which the dramatic information is being delivered (recitals of events
in ballad-meter; declarations of love in meters imitating those of the
fifteenth century songbooks). In the major writers we encounter no
separation of comedy and tragedy as understood outside the Spanish
dramatic tradition; sadness and clowning, deaths and marriages may
all appear in an individual play. Castillo, as we shall observe, comes

23

at a time when the purely comic play can be attempted, making him something of an outsider among Spanish dramatists.[3]

Where Castillo does conform to the standards of the mass of dramatists is, however, in his location of the mainsprings of the action of his plays in love and honor. "Love," it must be quickly pointed out in this theatrical context, is no especially noble passion but a totally banal accomplishment of desire, the realization of the dream of physical possession after predictable physical attraction. This love can hardly stimulate any character to accept higher ethical standards or reflect philosophically on the claims of the *other* upon the self. What it can do is degenerate effortlessly into jealousy and provide a dramatist like Castillo with a powerful secondary motivating force behind the plot. Whatever "honor" may be in the works of other authors, in Castillo it is purely the social projection of some masculine character's self-esteem, a tireless yearning to be more certain about what rivals and others are thinking on the subject of his worthiness. It is all very puerile. Where in the works of others there occur some savage scenes and resolutions on the part of characters in the matter of revenges due to a woman wronged, in Castillo typically there is nobody available to execute the vengeful act. Time and chance, as in his play *Outrage Atoned For,* have to perform the task of restoring a woman's honor in the only possible way—arranging for her eventual marriage to her seducer, at whatever cost to verisimilitude in characterization or in the observation of souls.

Behind every feature of the *comedia* stands a perennial convention, and this comes to our notice very strikingly in the matter of characters. There will usually be a father at least two generations older than his children, a gallant and a lady, a lady's confidant and servants of both sexes.[4] What will be lacking is any character recognizable as the mother of a family, but this convention as much as all the others proclaims the *comedia*'s ultimate origins in Roman comedy of antiquity, in the Latin dialogue *comoediae* of the Middle Ages and in Italian plays of the sixteenth century both spoken and in pantomime, that is, the *commedia dell'arte.*

We have referred in passing to the way in which every unserious *comedia* ends with the marriages of the gallant and the lady, and of their companions if these should be equals in social rank (and the plot call for their existence). A ludicrous extension of this convention is that the servant-characters, the *gracioso* and the *criada,* are obliged to follow suit and scramble into marriage with each other in the final scene. Since Castillo's plays make notable use of the jesting lackey or *gracioso* as a principal character, and since the comic lines spoken by such a character tend to be the only ones which redeem the weaker among the author's dramatic pieces, this type deserves a little closer study.[5]

I *The* Gracioso *As Type*

The nature of the *gracioso* is ultimately bound up with the contemporary "metaphysics" of social class as reflected in all literature. The *gracioso* inherits no noble blood, and no monarch can have possibly ennobled him, hence his creator cannot endow him with a character susceptible of any attraction towards the ideal or the pure. In contrast to his master the *galán*, he cannot spend his waking moments in pursuit of love and honor; he cannot even try to understand other characters' sensitivities about these things. He resides in the physical alone, and his only stimuli come from the everyday, the unpoetic, and what appeals to the grosser appetite.[6] On the other hand he can only exist within any particular play in conjunction with his nobler, more spiritual, more idealizing master, performing it must be said, most of the functions left to manservants outside the theater in those times as well as the more "poetic" role of rounding out the *galán*'s humanity, as though he were an earthy appanage forming a part of it. Each playwright of the Golden Age tended to conceive the *gracioso* in a different way, following his individual temperament or sense of audience. Castillo creates two distinct varieties: Gastón in *Outrage Atoned For* and Ruzafa in *The Specter of Valencia* (*La fantasma de Valencia*, 1634) correspond to the first type, the detached counselor and cynical commentator of soberer deportment, while Chilindrón in *Enchantments in Brittany* (*Los encantos de Bretaña*, 1634) and Chacota in *The Victory at Nördlingen* (*La victoria de Norlingen*, post-1634) act the other role, that of ludicrous, cowardly and voracious clowns. The names given to these latter characters denote their clownishness and ignobility.

Two *graciosos* of Castillo's, Marino in *The Lordly Buffoon* (*El mayorazgo figura*, 1639) and Fabio in *The Marquis from the Toledo Suburbs* (*El marqués del Cigarral*, 1634), have, it will be noticed, quite simple and non-ludicrous names. This is because they act their roles in plays which portray other figures of fun, the buffoons or *figurones,* and are necessarily eclipsed by these in the plots of the plays. Castillo has a certain predilection for this dramatic figure, and may even have harnessed a personal animus against ancient *hidalgo* (rural gentry's) privilege into his creation of the eccentric anti-*galán.* Where the *figurón* enters, the comic spirit of the piece (which in Castillo's hands can be fairly insipid) yields ground utterly to that of the farcical potential of a series of dramatic moments (and here Castillo, a master of the rhetoric of persiflage and invention of the scarcely human automata of the dramatic interlude, shows his supreme talent).

The first appearance of a *figurón* in a three-act play, setting aside the question of the prior creation of analogous figures in interludes, seems to occur in Lope de Vega's *The Bumpkin Gentry (Los hidalgos de aldea,* c. 1610), which presents us with the character Don Blas, who displays fantastic speech habits, ludicrously unfashionable clothing and an obsession with his pedigree.[7] After 1630, the public appears to have approved heartily of plays with these eccentrics as main characters, specifically when the plot concerns a betrothal.[8] Then the interest in the action settles itself around the danger the lady is in of ending up with the buffoon as her husband; Castillo amuses us by implying that through cupidity *(The Lordly Buffoon)* or a kind of boredom with an immature *galán (The Marquis from the Toledo Suburbs)* she might be tempted momentarily to go through with it.

There have been attempts to discern an ideological significance in the *figurónes,* with their distinctively unfashionable names: Lucas, Cosme, Blas, Fruela and the like, even a kind of policing by the rulers of Spain who authorized the *comedia,* of the incidence of anarchical singularity. The *figurón* canalizes onstage an urge towards nonconformity on the part of individualistic citizens,[9] while the implied enmity on the part of an impoverished nobleman like Castillo towards the ancient privileged *hidalgo* class is typically misdirected. Not country squires, but the likes of those laughing in the audience were the real architects of the ruin of *his* class. At least one might so hypothesize, somewhat by analogy with the drama of England in our own day where "class-conscious" playwrights rail at the titled aristocracy and present them as buffoons or *figurones,* while more identifiable "enemies of the people," by an oversight, never appear.

We should be on much firmer ground in proposing that the invention of such a character as the *figurón* (buffoon) is implicit in ancient comic theory. Quintilian, for instance, had remarked on the affinities of comedy with *ethos* (the immutable aspects of personality) as against tragedy's with *pathos* (the evanescence of passions and feelings). So it is that a grotesque eccentric can dominate a play, riding out the conflicts and tensions of the intrigue which so exert the non-eccentric humanity of the other characters.[10] Castillo's Don Cosme has learned nothing at the end of the play; there is no question of his character developing and, what is more, he could conceivably inhabit an infinite series of plays in the future just being himself.

II   El agravio satisfecho

Castillo's plays are fairly unfamiliar to modern students of the drama, so an account of their plots in chronological order will, it is hoped, isolate their characteristics. The dramatist began, so far as we know, with a romantic play, *Outrage Atoned For (El agravio satisfecho,* included in *La Huerta de Valencia,* 1629). Perhaps it was to Castillo's advantage that he passed so much time amid the patter of conversation in literary societies, for in *Outrage Atoned For* he is able to give the play a striking opening: the men-about-town of Seville are at their nocturnal ramblings, discussing women, when the conversation turns to the subject of noble delinquents, past and present, and the vexations these young men cause to their distinguished families. This serves to introduce the audience to Don Juan de Saavedra, whom they characterize as the reigning *valiente* or bully, and gamester. A certain Carranza, one of the company, is of the opinion that the best thing would be to dispatch him to Italy with the army, as a relief for Seville: "*Vaya a mostrar su valor a Nápoles o a Milán, que allá saben los soldados allanar desvanecidos, amansar los arriscados, humillar los presumidos y estimar a los honrados.*" ("Let him go to show his worth in Naples or in Milan. Because there the soldiers know how to bring down the vain to their true level, tame the overweening, humble those who are presumptuous, yet show esteem for the truly honorable.") [p. 230] Don Juan then turns up in person, accompanied by his valet Gastón,[11] to say goodbye before he in fact leaves for Naples. It is, however, unfortunate that the elderly Don Bernardo and his daughter María should alight from a coach at that moment to take a stroll, because Don

Juan profits from the occasion to carry her off in most brutal fashion. He has an explanation: "*Mi afición no se corrige a guiarse por razón. La mujer me ha enamorado . . . Yo la tengo de gozar o perder la vida en ello; . . .*" ("My inclination cannot be corrected so that reason guides it. The woman has aroused my love . . . I have to enjoy her or lose my life attempting it.") [pp. 237–38] The other gallants prudently remove themselves from the scene, leaving the poor Don Bernardo to make his eloquent lament all alone. Meanwhile in another part of the city the seduced and blindfolded María appears. She is being led about by the now inhumanly indifferent Don Juan: "*Quédate a Dios, que mejores mujeres he yo gozado que tú. Lástima me ha dado.*" ("Goodbye, for I have had better women than you. It has been pathetic.") [p. 243] To provide a poetic parallel to her father's speech of lamentation María deplores her fate at equal length. Later, arriving home, she offers a harrowing explanation of what has happened. There is one important detail: while in the darkened house to which she was taken she was able to secure a jewel which was lying in the bedroom. It is a chain with a pendant *agnus dei.*

The second act of *Outrage Atoned For* carries us to Italy and introduces us to Don Juan's excellent career in the army, undertaken in the company of a certain Don Vicente, with whom he has become acquainted. He still has his successes with women, even if we hear only of the high-society courtesan Julia. Gastón appears with a present which she has sent to Juan, providing an occasion for the hero to explain his intentions as far as Julia is concerned:

Juan: Nunca yo he tenido intento
de casar con esta dama;
galanteo solamente.

Gastón: Papel, favor y presente
¿no disminuyen su fama?

Vicente: Gastón dice bien, don Juan.
Gastón: Que lo demás es engaño.

Juan: I have never had any intention of marrying that lady. I'm merely carrying on an affair.

Gastón: A letter, a favorable attitude and a present from her; don't these damage her reputation?

Vincente: Gastón is right, Juan.
Gastón: Trickery is the name for the rest of what you're doing.

Vicente: Y aun podéis temer un daño, según las cosas están de Nápoles; . . .	Vincente: And you might even be wary of a physical attack on you, considering how things are at Naples.

(p. 259)

Meanwhile a child has been born to María, and she and Don Bernardo see fit to leave it with peasants outside Seville. Don Bernardo, however, all the time is sinking into poverty; in spite of his noble lineage he is unable to obtain the credit he once could. The peasant foster-father arrives to complain about not getting his allowance and also to surmise that María is the mother: "*Si ella acaso lo parió—que lo pienso a mi entender—pues nada pudo perder, ¿por qué no se lo crió? Hacen sus malos recados y con decir 'pagaremos' pretenden que lo lastemos los labradores cuitados.*" ("If she perchance gave birth to it—and I think so, on reflexion—since she had nothing to lose, why didn't she bring it up? These people make their mistakes, and then, saying "We shall pay," they expect us peasants, for whom life is hard, to bear the burden.") [p. 268] In spite of the protests of Hipólito, Don Bernardo's man of confidence, made out of an impecunious loyalty (perhaps explicable because Hipólito follows Castillo's own profession of servitor to the nobility), father and daughter are obliged to find the money or their secret will come out. Then out of the blue comes the recollection of Don Sebastián de Saavedra,[12] a man renowned for his generosity towards distressed gentlefolk, and they go to visit him. Don Bernardo has to provide Don Sebastián with an account of his life and misfortunes (and luckily has acquired another creditor to cite as his pretext for asking for a loan). He offers as collateral the chain and *agnus dei,* and of course Don Sebastián recognizes it as the one his son once owned. Faced with Don Sebastián's curiosity Don Bernardo has to tell more, about his son Vicente now with the army in Naples and finally about the rape and abandonment of María. A marriage is then immediately planned.

Castillo provides some very effective moments of dramatic suspense as everyone awaits the return of Don Juan—coincidentally now a very changed man. Even Don Bernardo has now to admire the paragon who appears: "*Bizarro mozo es, por Dios, y ha dado en*

Italia muestras, en lo bélico y brioso, de su sangre y su nobleza."
("He is, in God's name, a spirited young man, and he's given an
example in Italy of his blood and his nobility by his prowess and his
mettle.") [p. 299] There occurs at this point Castillo's only gesture
towards providing this play with an underplot, as the servants Gastón and Costanza make fun of Don Sebastián's *major-domo*
Calatayud, a personage very like Shakespeare's Malvolio. But really
little is left to resolve in this final scene other than the reconcilia-
tions of Vicente and Don Bernardo—for indeed Vicente was that
very lost son—and of María and her erstwhile brutal violator who
declaims Garcilaso de la Vega's immortal line:" *Oh dulces prendas,
por mi mal halladas!"* ("Oh sweet tokens, reappearing to make me
sad!") over the chain and the *agnus dei.*

III   Sources and Parallels

Several works of Spanish literature in the Golden Age will have
suggested themselves to the reader of the above summary as having
close affinities. First, there is Cervantes's exemplary novel *The
Power of Blood* (*La fuerza de la sangre*, 1613), which also depends
on the device of a rape by an unknown assailant, who is betrayed
later by a jewel secured in the darkness by the girl. There is the
same conversion of the violator after a sojourn in Italy, though what
effects the conversion is never clear in either case. It could be the
occult action of the *agnus dei* on its true owner, or it could be the
metaphysical result of Don Juan's exertions in his military capacity.
In this latter case we would have to compare what happens with
what is predicted as likely to happen in Garcilaso de la Vega's *Second Eclogue* to the violent lover Albanio after the apprenticeship of
his soul in martial pursuits.[13] A variant of this plot was also used by
Calderón de la Barca in his *There's Nothing Like Staying Silent* (*No
hay cosa como callar* of 1638 or 1639) in which, however, the jewel
is given a much more decisive influence on the outcome of the plot,
and no unsatisfactory coincidences strike the spectator as with Castillo.[14] The main character of Calderón's play is also called Don
Juan, and it might be interesting to consider both plays as themati-
cally associated with the great seventeenth century Spanish drama
The Trickster of Seville (*El burlador de Sevilla*) first printed in the
year following Castillo's, 1630. Castillo brings out the brutality in his
Don Juan rather than the penchant for provoking social and ethical

chaos attributable to Don Juan Tenorio; that is, Castillo endows him with a remediable fault. But other aspects of the play seem to have their echoes: the geographical axis Naples-Seville; the jester-companion (Catalinón in *The Trickster of Seville*) who tries to call the deceiver to order; the sheer alacrity of both Don Juans, in each case thrown into relief against an assemblage of talkative, nerveless and erotically indolent gallants. Quite apart from these parallels Castillo's play has an intrinsic interest as a document of its epoch and of the general pattern of its author's thought, especially in the matter of money and its effects on the characters and actions of Bernardo, María and Don Juan.

IV   Los encantos de Bretaña

When we come to Castillo's next play, *Enchantments in Brittany*, it must be stated first of all that the plot has nothing to do with the medieval French Arthurian romance *Enchantements de Bretagne*. The play is a pretext in large part for the accumulation of transformation effects and fantastic spectacular flights through the air above the scenery.[15] Duke Arnaldo of Aquitaine is the object of the affections of two noble ladies, Arminda, Princess of Brittany, and Laura, Duchess of some unspecified territory. Each lady commands the services of an enchanter, and this leads to much sudden transportation over land and sea of the Duke and his crude but eloquent valet Chilindrón. The Duke has no occult advantage such as the ladies have, knows no specific against enchantment, and consequently passes much time mystified, terrified or merely depressed. A subplot concerns the covetousness of the Admiral, who has a desire for the throne to which Arminda is heiress, and the fairly tepid love of Enrico, his son, for Arminda as a person. The two plots are joined fortuitously by Ardano, Arminda's enchanter, who plays a double game and is, indeed, quite unconcerned himself as to who shall attain to the throne of Brittany.

It would be unprofitable to follow all the turns of the plot while the scenery is transformed from forest to castle interior and again to seacoast, mostly at the magical behest of Ardano. The magician is, however, successful in inclining Arnaldo's affections at last towards Arminda. By the third act, Laura has succeeded in her turn in fraying Arnaldo's nerves if nothing else, and it would be even worse if he were in possession of the information that she has urged the

King of France to arrest him as guilty of breach of promise. All the involuntary aerial journeys have their effect: Arnaldo and Chilindrón end up execrating Laura and admitting their terror of her. The miserable Arnaldo says he wishes he might be born again, if his present life would only end, and this leads to a most curious discourse by Chilindrón on what the unborn and the newly-born must experience:

Chilindrón: ¿Estás acaso en tu
acuerdo—
porque pienso que
deliras?
¿Nacer de nuevo deseas
a este mundo? No
imaginas
en el recién engendrado
las pasiones infinitas
que padece sin ver luz.

Duque: Eso quiero que me digas.

Chilindrón: Dejemos las circun-
stancias—
pues que no son para
dichas—
que hay hasta que es
engendrado
el embrión que se anima.
¿Es muy gustoso habitar
la alcoba de una barriga,
rodeado de un mondongo,
cercado de su inmundicia?
¿Es gustoso ya crecido
el estar siempre en
cuclillas,
apartando con las manos
que se hagan allá las
tripas?
¿Es gustoso al darse
anchura
tener con el bazo riñas,
con el hígado pendencias,
con el obispillo grita?
¿Es bueno estar esperando
el sustento boca arriba,

Are you by chance in
your right mind? Because
I'm thinking you're
delirious. You want to
be born again into this
world? You can't imagine
the endless pains
experienced by the
newly-begotten infant
before he sees the light.
I'd like you to explain
that.
Let's leave aside the
circumstances—since
they aren't for repeating—
which precede the conception
of the embryo. Do you think
it's fun to inhabit the alcove
of a belly, hemmed in by an
intestine and surrounded by
its soil? Do you think it's fun
once growth has begun, to be
always squatting, pushing the
entrails aside with your
hands? Do you think it's fun
when you stretch to do battle
with the spleen, fight a duel
with the liver and brawl with
the popesnose? Do you think
it's fun to remain waiting
for your food mouth upwards,
and to find that those victuals
are what
didn't rub off on the shift?
Do you think it's fun to emerge
pushed rudely into the light

y que el tal sustento sea
lo que faltó a las camisas?
¿Es bien salir a empujones
a luz, y que te reciba
una comadre en espera
envuelto entre las orinas,
con el rostro carilargo,
con la nariz carichica
y la cabeza más chata
que pomo de espada
	antigua?
¿Es gusto llorar por teta
con tiple de chinfonía
y si no quieres dormir
que el coco te ponga
	grimas?
¿Es gusto el sufrir que
	una ama,
si es gallega una cantiña,
y si acaso no la sabe,
el cantar la lalalila?
¿Es gusto al nacer los
	dientes
que te duelan las encías,
y que entonces te den
	papas
por fuerza con cucharita?
¿Es bueno el ponerte
	trabas
para andar todos los días?
¿Y es gustoso andar con
	miedo
a gatas o a arrimadillas?
¿Es bueno que un
	sarampión
te acometa y que te rinda,
y después unas viruelas
te dejen hecho una criba?
¿Es bien si llega el
	invierno
que con sus escarchas rizas
te te cubras de sabañones,
fruta que de andar te
	priva?

and, covered in urine, to be
received by a waiting midwife,
with your elongated face, your
squashed nose and your head
more flattened than the pommel
of an ancient sword? Is it fun
to cry for the breast with a
squeak like a bagpipe and, if
you don't want to sleep, for
the bogey to make faces at you?
Is it fun when your nursemaid,
if she is a Gallegan, sings a
song of her people, or if
she perhaps can't sing one, chants
the Morisco's Islamic prayer?
Is it fun,
when your teeth appear, for your
gums to hurt and for people to
force pap into you with a spoon?
Is it so good when you're put
into a walking-frame every day?
And
is it pleasant to go fearfully
on all fours or holding on to
things? Is it nice when an
attack of measles overcomes
you, and later the chickenpox
leaves you looking like a sieve?
Is it so pleasant when winter
comes with its hoarfrosts that
you should be covered with
chilblains, that fruit which
won't allow you to walk? If,
considering all these
disadvantages, it still tempts
you to want to be born again,
well, you've got a depraved
taste and—you'll have
people laughing at you.

Si con aquestas pensiones
volver a nacer te inclina
el gusto tiénesle malo,
y harás que de ti se rían.

The customary marriages terminate this play: Arnaldo to Arminda, since he had not sought to employ magical arts to secure her, and Enrico to the imperious Laura, apparently because he had taken that course. Though the plot is in truth negligible, the dialogue which Castillo has provided is never flaccid, and this seems to be a constant with him. We have no record that *Enchantments in Brittany* was ever staged, although an audience easily impressed by the effects of stage-machinery could have applauded it.

V   La fantasma de Valencia

Though Castillo claims that the play next in date, *The Specter of Valencia (La fantasma de Valencia)*, dramatizes a portion of the family saga of the Marradas (the same clan whose adulation he attempts, also to little avail, in *The Victory at Nördlingen*) what we have is the putting together of many triturated elements of stories of high romance. Castillo has a prose novella with the same title, but this is no more than a coincidence, and moreover the apparition of the title refers to a whole illusionistic technique onstage rather than to a single ghost's appearance.

Castillo opens his play with a scene more typical of the interlude: indolent gallants are strolling by night in the streets of Valencia. It is St. John's Eve and ladies are also about, seeking to test the superstitious belief that the first passerby when asked will bear the same name as the future betrothed. Don Juan, Don Diego and the *gracioso* Ruzafa spoil all this by giving facetious replies such as "Don Quixote" and "Sancho Panza." After commenting on various other ladies who live nearby, the gallants retire. Not long afterward, however, Don Juan and Ruzafa reappear to take part in a most crowded scene, the result of which is to inform the audience, it now being morning, that the lady Teodora has been rescued from the sea by yet another gallant, Don Leandro. Her coach had been driven into the sea by a negligent coachman.[16] A side-effect is that now Don Juan feels the incentive to press his attentions with a little more ardor on Teodora, hoping to abandon unobtrusively in the process his previous obligations to his own lady, Laura. Before the end of the act, there occurs a scene in which all four of these aspirants, gallants and ladies, actually meet amid predictable emotional tensions. These are allowed to exhaust themselves for the moment, and very unjustly, in the dismissal by Teodora of her Moorish confidante, Celima. What the other characters do not know, of course, is that Celima has magical powers and can make things appear as they are not whenever she chooses. Much of the rest of the play will concern the stage effects made possible by these powers of transformation.

The second act is largely made up of the interplay of scenes in which the "real" and "phantom" versions of Don Juan, Teodora and—for the purposes of the negligible subplot—her maid Juana promote false assignations, a complete ball in progress onstage which disappears in an instant, and horrendous jealousies and remorse.[17] Swordplay between Don Leandro and the real Don Juan results from a rather good scene in which the real Teodora is discovered in bed sleeping after another "Teodora" had been locked into a closet. When nothing is found behind the closet door, misunderstandings begin to be cleared up, and Celima appears, to ask for forgiveness—and baptism. She prophesies that a nephew of the family will achieve military renown with the Emperor Ferdinand.

VI   El marqués del Cigarral

One of Castillo's more durable and influential plays is *The Marquis from the Toledo Suburbs (El marqués del Cigarral)*, one which had great success, whether in spite of or because of a pronounced conflict of classes implicit in its theme. In the town of Orgaz we are introduced to the typical, stupid gallant of Castillo's comedy, Don Antonio, explaining to his man Fabio that he cannot detach himself from Leonor, even though this girl is a mere commoner. We also hear of the comedy's buffoon *(figurón)* Don Cosme de Armenia, who pretends to great nobility but convinces nobody: "A gentleman from an oblique angle, a wellborn clodhopper" *("caballero . . . al soslayo, un villano . . . bien nacido")*. However, everyone of any importance tolerates Don Cosme, despite his follies.

This is well elucidated when Cosme appears, talking to a simple country magistrate *(alcalde)*, reminding him that he is related to no less a personage than the Emperor Charles V, through Japhet, their common ancestor. That is, Don Cosme is making the attempt, since the *alcalde* can understand very little indeed of the verbiage of his noble interlocutor. The polarization of the aristocracy at the time of this play between those who were becoming grandees (*grandes de España*) and those who, like Castillo himself, were being forced down among the commonalty, peeps out in Cosme's reply:

Alcalde: ¿Qué es grande [de España]?	Mayor: What is there to being a Spanish grandee?
Cosme: Forrar meollo con fieltro y tafetán liso delante del Emperador.	Cosme: It consists in stuffing the insides with felt and smooth taffeta, in the Emperor's presence. (B.A.E., p. 310)

Don Antonio and Fabio are worked back into the plot of the comedy by means of their inclusion, in disguise, in a parade of prospective servants for Don Cosme's household. The relation of this scene to the several parade-interludes by Castillo is obvious. Don Antonio secures a post as "secretary,"[18] while his valet becomes Cosme's "*major-domo*", but the fact that Antonio has "stooped to conquer" has not removed the real obstacle to the fulfillment of his love for Leonor: the social one. This complication, indeed, becomes urgent when Cosme, in the course of hearing a description of the amenities of Orgaz, now learns of the existence of Leonor as well. He becomes so enthusiastic that he proposes at once to take her over—as though by right—as his mistress, but the situation is saved when a letter is read out by the Alcalde which proves that Leonor was actually born into a noble family:

Leonor: ¡Haberme dado esta dicha los cielos, naciendo noble, de prosapia ilustre y limpia!	To think that heaven conferred this blessing on me, to be of noble birth and of brilliant and unsullied pedigree!
Cosme: . . . Ya olvido el concubinato; aun pensarlo es grosería.	I'm already discarding thoughts of a mere liaison; even to consider it is vile. (B.A.E., p. 314)

The second act introduces what amounts to a new play, but Castillo purposely left the first action with some arbitrary loose ends to be tied up. The rest of the comedy concerns the unmasking of the *figurón* Don Cosme at the instigation of two noble pranksters, the Grand Prior (of a military order of knighthood) and Don Íñigo, proprietor of a *cigarral*, that is, one of the suburban villas, with extensive grounds, close to the city of Toledo. Since these two—reminiscent of Don Álvaro Tarfe and Don Carlos in Fernández de Avellaneda's *Second Part of Don Quixote* (1614) in more than one respect—are back from the Emperor's court in Italy, the prank is to consist of telling Don Cosme that he has been awarded, by Charles V himself, and out of the blue, a marquisate. The bogus letters-patent include the formal address of *primo* (cousin); Cosme, of course, concludes that he has been recognized as a scion of the House of Habsburg itself, and so invents imaginary military exploits which have entitled him to the honor of becoming Marqués del Cigarral. The point about the title is that *cigarras* (cicadas) are the equivalent of "bees in the bonnet," whatever may have been the origin of the topographical term.[19] Cosme describes, still in his ludicrous style, how he will improve his marquisate and quite forgets about Leonor until he is reminded.

This is a good point in the play for the question of the misapprised social circumstances of Antonio and Leonor to be cleared up, even though our gallant has to admit that he was on the way to Seville to meet and marry Matilde, a rich half-Aztec lady, daughter of a chief *(cacique)*. Cosme surprises "his secretary" kissing Leonor's hand, and is furious. At this point it is revealed that the Grand Prior and Don Íñigo were looking for Antonio, and had assumed either that he was dead or was spying on his bride-to-be incognito in Seville. The thought of Matilde prompts Antonio to keep up his pretense a little longer. Bullfights are announced, and also a prank to be played on Cosme. This begins with the traditional prank of inducing him to climb up a ropeladder to Leonor's room, only to find a shut window. Íñigo pretends he has apprehended a burglar and threatens to stone the protesting "grandee." They make him disarm and undress, however, and a duenna empties a slop pail over him. When the watch arrests him he is obliged to claim that he has been swimming.

The matchmaking interest resumes with Antonio in the dilemma of not wishing to reveal himself to Íñigo, even though he learns that his mother is fearful that he is dead. This is resolved when Íñigo

overhears Antonio and Leonor anyway. First he is indignant, but
then capitulates in the face of youthful love. Cosme's intervention in
the bullfight is entirely disastrous and ludicrous, as we of course
hear. He is furious about Antonio's match, but gets Matilde as a
compensation. She is at this point described as from the Inca capital
of Cuzco, where there never were "Aztec chieftains," of course, but
this is a comedy.

El marqués del Cigarral (The Marquis from the Toledo Suburbs)
is Castillo's best play, with satirical and motivational interests of a
high order. It merited immediate adaptation into French by Thomas
Corneille *(Dom Bertrand de Cigarral)* and Paul Scarron *(Dom
Japhet d'Arménie),* but its progeny among the works of Molière
himself and the English Restoration dramatists are its true posterity.

VII   El mayorazgo figura

The Lordly Buffoon (El mayorazgo figura) is a light-hearted comedy of some distinction, a sort of "taming of the shrew," in this case,
the mercenary Elena. At the beginning of the play Diego is hoping
to marry Elena, but cannot be sure about the fortune said to be
coming to him by sea. In a subsequent scene we encounter the rival
lady, Leonor, who has been in love with him ever since he rescued
her from a burning house, though she admits that she is not unaware
of his monetary expectations and has herself, as it happens, a portion
of six thousand ducats to bestow. We hear cursorily of a certain Don
Juan whom it is important that they avoid. The reason soon becomes
clear when Juan is discovered pursuing Leonor right into Elena's
house. Fortunately Diego appears and explains that he will actually
help Juan if he will try to be courteous, so inevitably Juan absents
himself from the play for a long time. There is a ridiculous scene in
which Leonor visits Diego and tries to make him doubt the wisdom
of courting Elena any longer. Meanwhile, Diego's fortune is still at
sea, so his servant Marino,[20] conceives a plan: he will impersonate
the "real" heir to the money, to expose the covetousness of Elena.

And so it is that in Act Two Diego produces a letter for Elena to
read which declares a certain cousin of Diego's, Don Payo from
remote Galicia, to be the heir. Elena immediately shows an interest
in this Don Payo. The entry of Marino in disguise is, of course, one
of the funniest scenes in the comedy: Castillo has him express himself in *culto* verbiage, punctuated by the catch-phrase *(baldón)*

"Isn't that so, Hermenegildo?" over and over again. He lists the costly presents shipped from the Indies, by their Indian names. Nobody is impressed, except Elena, with this *"marido figura / de los tiempos de Rodrigo / de Vivar. . . ."* ("this farcical husband from the days of the Cid Rodrigo de Vivar"). The rest of the act merely marks time, as Juan reappears, to take an interest in Leonor (though Elena will, we find, do for him just as well). The third act merely provides the obvious resolution or *desenlace:* the final convincing of the obstinate Diego of Leonor's superiority after the unmasking of "Payo," the *mayorazgo figura.* The weddings—of Diego to Leonor and of Juan to Elena—predictably terminate the play.

It is no accident that the farcical, interlude-style scenes are Castillo's most successful in this comedy. He has a certain grasp of the comedy of humors, so that the mercenary Elena gets the surly Juan as a mate, but the capacity for constructing charming gallants and ladies expected of a comic dramatist is evidently beyond Castillo's ability here. Diego seems merely stupid and Leonor sly.

VIII   La torre de Florisbella

Although *Florisbella's Tower (La torre de Florisbella,* 1640) received by some accident two editions, it surely can never have been performed. It may be properly considered an extravaganza requiring complicated stage-machines *(tramoyas).* Indeed, at a certain point one of the *graciosos* (for this play has two) ridicules quite effectively even the kind of play he is cast in:

Trapaza: A ser poeta novicio, destos que cursan tramoyas, vuelos y otros requisitos intrusos en la comedia, era aqueste asunto lindo para hacer una de fama, con seguridad de silbos.	If it were a case of a beginner among playwrights —one of those who employ stage-machines, flying wires and other uncalled-for equipment in the drama—this would be a very nice subject about which to construct a famous piece —with the certainty of its being whistled off the stage.

(p. 299)

The plot derives from high romance, employing one of high romance's most cherished openings: a shipwreck. The agitated deck of a ship is brought into our view, a scene which resembles that of the one which opens Shakespeare's *Tempest,* and there is much use of wires and similar mechanical aids. Prince Felisardo of Naples and his man Trapaza are cast ashore, and the latter declaims:

Dicha ha sido llegar adonde estamos,	It has been a piece of
oh gran piélago, círculo del orbe,	good luck to get to where
que naves traga, que galeras sorbe,	we are, oh great ocean,
teatro de ballenas y caimanes,	encircler of the world,
almacén de traidores huracanes—	you who swallow ships and
que el menor dellas chupa	drag down galleys, scene
como si fuera guinda una chalupa—	of action of whales and
pues de ti me he escapado,	crocodiles, warehouse of
ojos no me verán más embarcado.	treacherous hurricanes—
	for the smallest whale
	sucks in a sloop as if it
	were a cherry—since I
	have escaped from you, no
	eye will ever see me
	again aboard a ship.
	(pp. 271–72)

Still hewing to the pattern of high romance, Castillo introduces yet another prince and his servant, of entirely comparable character and disposition. The English reader might think here of the duplicated heroes of romance in, say, Sidney's *Arcadia.* Here in Castillo's play Lusidoro, a French prince, and his servant Perinola arrive carried by a gryphon to the same island of the shipwreck. At their meeting the two princes explain their itineraries: Felisardo, having lost his lady to the Duke of Amalfi, had resolved on revenge, but a mysterious voice led him aboard an enchanted ship, the one which was wrecked. For his part, Lusidoro was out hunting and after following and killing a boar was whisked away by the gryphon.

The lonely men try to make a boat and oars out of nearby trees, but one beech tree groans when it is cut in two and out of it comes Clarinda, lady-in-waiting to two daughters of the magician king of the isle, Calidorante. The arrival of the princes of the island is then no longer a mystery; magical arts have been employed to procure sons-in-law for this monarch. Clarinda leads the four men along a dark, subterranean gallery, a scene which is curiously converted into a really amusing burlesque of night-scenes in the *comedia*. Such scenes were, after all, rather new inventions and, as it happens in this play, very useful occasions for concealing the preparations for upcoming activity with the sophisticated stage-machinery.

The two princesses have, it appears, made their choices among the two involuntary suitors, so that the rest of the play revolves around mistaken envy of Felisardo on the part of Lusidoro, and rather pointless pretexts for the use of *tramoyas* such as the tower of the title, which may be opened by anyone holding a magic bough, and is capable of flying away by itself. Except that this leads to a situation in which Lusidoro is usefully carried off the scene, when Castillo can think of no other way of protracting the action, little is added to the plot by the scenes involving the tower.

Lusidoro's complaint when he learns that he is disdained (as he puts it) by Florisbella is worthy of attention, since it reveals a good deal about the entirely adolescent mentality of Castillo's *galanes,* while all the while projected seriously towards the audience as an illustration of his "nobility":

Tropiezo en el desengaño	I stumble against disillusion in
de mi amor, y es el tropiezo	my love, and the scandal is to see
veros en ajenos brazos,	you in someone else's arms and
y que tengáis gusto en ellos.	that you take pleasure in them.
¿Es Felisardo más noble	Is Felisardo more noble than I?
que yo? ¿Tiene más aumentos	Has he greater advantages of
de calidad, ni de estados?	lineage or of state? As regards
En cuanto al valor y esfuerzo	bravery and effort, has he any
¿tiéneme algunas ventajas?	superiority over me? So, since I
Pues si lo mismo que él tengo,	have the same as he, and even
y aun algo más, que conocen	somewhat more in the view of
desapasionados pechos,	disinterested judges, why has he
¿por qué es a mí preferido	been preferred to me, in the
con la elección que habéis hecho?	choice you have made?

(p. 310)

The magic bough operates to allow Trapaza to make his own way into the tower to surprise the sleeping Clarinda. The stage-machinery, however, drops a lion on to him and he prudently flees from the scene. From this point in the play there is singularly little to retain the reader's (as distinct from the unsophisticated spec-

tator's) attention. We encounter, it is true, one of Castillo's more
inspired burlesques of *culto* versifying:

Clarinda: ¿Qué es culto?	What is *"culto"*?
Trapaza: Una jerigonza que los mismos que la hablan son aquellos que la ignoran.	A jargon which those very ones who speak it are ignorant of.
Clarinda: Deseo oír algo della.	I should like to hear a little of it.
Trapaza: Pues con atención me oiga: "Mansión apolínea indica luz no, visibles antorchas sí, que dominando algentes, con nada se parangonan".	Then listen to me carefully: "The Apollinean dwellings do not so much indicate light as those visible torches which, lording it pitilessly, are incomparable."
Clarinda: Eso ¿qué quiere decir?	What does that all mean?
Trapaza: Hablando en culto idioma, que son tus ojos divinos luces de esa clara zona.	In *culto* idiom it means that your heavenly eyes are the lights of that bright region.

(p. 337)

To bring the play to a close, Castillo arranges nothing less than a
tournament onstage between two *galanes*, who hope to attain—by
winning—the favors of their destined ladies. It would be no real
tournament without *letras* (mottoes), and Castillo has a little fun by
punning at the end with these, introducing a *letrado* (attorney) of
comic interlude type to substantiate, quite incoherently, that particular play on words.

And so we are conducted back into the frame story of *The Salon*.
*Se representó muy bien, se adornó con muchas galas y los torneantes
lo hicieron bizarramente.* ("It was well acted, it was adorned with
much finery and the champions in the tournament acquitted themselves well.") Perhaps the saddest thing about this drama, or rather
pretext for setting wires and windlasses into motion, is the uncom-

prehending misappropriation of the venerable phenomena of folklore, such as the speaking tree, the magic bough, or even the mystagogic wild boar. These fragments of ancient fairy lore are hurled into the text by Castillo quite unfeelingly, as so many more ingredients in the spectacle he is purveying. Thus it is that they lose their primordial power to evoke the magical and the numinous.

IX   La victoria de Norlingen

The Victory of Nördlingen, or The Infante in Germany (La victoria de Norlingen y el Infante en Alemania) is a work in which Castillo extracts a preposterous series of situations from incidents attending the historical Battle of Nördlingen in the Thirty Years' War. The first scene introduces us to the anti-imperial, and therefore anti-Spanish generals Gustavo Horn and the Duke of Weimar. They are shown as friendly colleagues, though the historical personages with those names were highly mistrustful of each other. The play opens with Weimar reviewing the situation of the war, and Castillo incongruously has him do this purely from the Imperialists' point of view. He has no words of praise for his own officers, while he singles out the activities of the Valencian general Marradas on the other side as meritorious. This officer is hardly recorded in histories of the Thirty Years' War as more than a "pacifier" and garrison commander in Bohemia, but Castillo seems to have been a client of the family.

The lady *(dama)*, the servant *(criada)*, the gallant *(galán)* and the jester *(gracioso)* immediately appear, to introduce the romantic possibilities of the play. Andalisa, maidservant of Laura, Weimar's sister, announces the arrival of two strangers whom the audience knows to be the Duke of Lorraine and his Spanish sergeant Chacota. Although he does not divulge his name—and nobody asks him to—Lorraine is offered a colonelcy by Weimar, who praises him as "worthy of being a Spaniard!"[21] We also hear the complicated story of why Lorraine has exiled himself from France along with his "young brother."

Interest moves back to the war and the advance of the Habsburg King of Hungary on Nördlingen (historically an operation commanded by the less blueblooded General Gallas) towards the camp of the Spanish Cardinal-Infante. From this point these two princely commanders, both called Fernando, will act as one character in the drama. Castillo's patrons, the Marradas family, merit further mention here. Some relevant facts are provided in the report made to the Cardinal-Infante by his subordinate Diego Mesía; unfortunately it refers to unrelated skirmishes in Bohemia where Marradas was, in fact, active. Back in Weimar's camp, there is suspense as Andalisa convinces her mistress that Lorraine's "brother" is actually a lady disguised. The pointlessly jealous Laura has violent thoughts, but amid all this Lorraine and Chacota (and presumably the disguised lady) make off towards the imperialist lines.

In the second act, Lorraine appears before the Cardinal-Infante and explains once more his persecution by the hateful Richelieu in his native land, his flight with his wife, but *not* his visit to Weimar's camp. Chacota identifies himself as a man of Segovia, from Zamarramala, a name which perhaps was in itself ludicrous in Castillo's time, but from which the humor has now evaporated.[22] A change of scene brings before us a changed Weimar, now almost an overweening braggart soldier, confident that the impending arrival of the forces of the Rheingrave Otto-Ludwig will give him the necessary superiority to storm Nördlingen. Horn is made to suggest the attack on the overlooking Weinberg, though the historical Swedish general was diffident at that point, aware that his side had only some fifteen to twenty thousand men to the imperialists' thirty-five to forty thousand (of whom some ten thousand were Spanish).[23]

For details of the battle ensuing, Castillo obviously relies on news reports which certainly follow the main incidents in the correct order, though there seems historically to have been no major attack by night and in a storm, as in the play. The Spanish infantry were never in any real danger of being dislodged by the progressively weaker Swedish onslaughts. No dramatic use is made, either, of a memorable incident in which the Cardinal-Infante was able to destroy in a cavalry charge a major Swedish position already in confusion after the accidental explosion of the defenders' powder.[24] Castillo's Weimar would like to evacuate his sister Laura from the field, but she wishes to take part in the action to emulate "her relative" the Queen of Sweden. The historical Christina of Sweden—and it must be she who is meant—was only eight years old at the time of Nördlingen and, of course, the Dukes of Weimar were purely German allies, not Swedish.

The dramatist returns us to scenes of love in a peaceful forest nearby, where Lorraine has gone to sleep with his wife's portrait in his hand, while Chacota snores by his side. Laura, on her arrival there, most presumptuously substitutes her own portrait for that of Lorraine's beloved. Andalisa, for her part, stains Chacota's face hideously with the juices of nearby weeds. Lorraine does at least awaken in time to see Laura leave, but nothing follows from this scene. The rest of the act is warlike and taken up with the representation of the assault on the Weinberg, accompanied by much noise and nocturnal havoc, while Weimar declaims in rage like a kind of ogre against the success of the Spanish forces.[25] Laura and Andalisa lose their way on the battlefield, and so does Chacota, who is carrying a box of jewels he has found. They all stray into the Imperialist camp, and Laura, challenged by the King of Hungary, is forced to tell a lie.

The third act produces the actual meeting of Lorraine and Laura, just before the final daylight attack. Andalisa is also rescued in a crassly amusing scene, from a brutal anti-Imperialist soldier, by Chacota. The attack succeeds and Imperialist casualties are estimated at only five hundred, while the Swedish side loses sixteen thousand (historically, they lost ten thousand, and four thousand taken prisoner with Horn). Until the fleeing Weimar can be found Lorraine, in the unexplained absence of his wife, retains the custody of Laura. Castillo, to be fair to him, does imply that the princely commanders did not in fact contribute much towards the defeat of Weimar in the field, although Werth, the officer who actually routed him, goes unnamed.

The dramatist's reliance on news-relations is not to blame for the faulty dramaturgy of this play. Except for the *gracioso* Chacota and his counterpart Andalisa, not a single character seems to be adequately motivated. The Infante of the play's subtitle is represented as a desk general owing a great deal of his tactics to the initiative of the outsider Lorraine.[26] Laura, although the *dama*, makes herself ridiculous, first by presuming without evidence that Lorraine loves her and then by importuning him instead of finding out about his married state. Castillo, finally, does not really know what to do with Weimar, and to avoid his assimilation to the character of the tragic hero, defeated both by fate and a more numerous enemy, he transforms him into a kind of demoniac. We do not hear that the play was ever performed. If it was, the effects suggesting lightning-flashes and artillery-fire must have counted for much.

X   El fuego dado del cielo

Quite recently a Corpus Christi play in one act *(auto sacramental)*
has been edited for the first time, and attributed to Castillo's period
of religious writings, around 1635 and 1636.[27] It is *The Fire Sent
from Heaven (El fuego dado del cielo)*, not an allegorical play but
one presenting Biblical personages: Daniel and Nehemiah as lead-
ers of the Jews in exile, Cyrus and Darius as Assyrian potentates,
and one Biblical episode: the restoration of Jerusalem after the
miraculous gift of fire. Castillo provides an inconsequential love-in-
terest: the rivalry of Cyrus and Darius for Rosa and Florinda, and a
gracioso Zabulón, both a stout champion of Judaism and a humorous
connecting link between the various scenes taken eclectically from
the Scriptures. In a final scene there is a vision of the Christ Child,
which helps to equate, metaphysically, charity with the "fire sent
from heaven."

CHAPTER 4

The Novel of the Ingenious Fraud

THE most sustained narratives of Castillo Solórzano are those usually classified as his "picaresque novels." Since there has been a certain confusion in the criticism of recent decades with reference to the picaresque genre perhaps a working definition of it, applicable almost exclusively to the examples found in the Spanish Golden Age, might conveniently preface our discussion. It is a body of ingenious narratives in prose, normally recounted in the first person singular, concerning the lives and adversities of certain individuals living in the humbler ranks of society, and patterned as a sequence of episodes: accounts of service rendered to several masters or encounters with diverse people. The whole fiction, in any one case, will be conditioned by the nature of the protagonist (the *pícaro*) and by the associations which he (sometimes she) may make. The series of episodes tends to satirize society; the language of this satire is invariably eloquent, never unlearned.[1] Clearly this characterization of the picaresque applies best to the foremost example, Mateo Alemán's *Guzmán de Alfarache* (1599; 1604). It cannot, we hope to show convincingly, be made to fit the works of Castillo, even though these characterizations may portray the activities of similarly ignoble personages. In Castillo's books these activities are exclusively practical jokes and ingenious frauds and consequently, those narratives might much more accurately be called novels of swindling. Episodes of adversity or of employment by a master are, in them, actually only trampolines serving to project the character—who is, incidentally, in only one instance presented in the first person singular—in the direction of further ingenious frauds, relieved by ingenious and often callous practical jokes.

The earliest of these narratives of Castillo's is a short one: "The Proteus of Madrid" ("*El Proteo de Madrid*," in *Tardes entretenidas*, 1625). Here the chief character is Domingo, who has begun his life as a child abandoned by his Galician mother in Madrid. By good fortune he enters an excellent foster home, in spite of which his inherited mischievous inclination comes into the open. The rest of the brief story concerns itself with Domingo's practical jokes and swindles, though we must not omit the fact that he himself is occasionally swindled in turn. Towards the end he is robbed by his scheming female companion, later attempts to impersonate an old woman in order to deceive almsgivers, and is punished by being sent to the galleys. In this short novel, it is obvious that the episodes themselves are of greater moment than the development of Domingo's character or any cautionary intention on Castillo's part. The episodes are offered as being essentially unserious, so that the lie is given to the perfunctory preliminary declarations that there is a moral to this tale. Perhaps we ought to attach such a work, segmented into its funny episodes, to the tradition of the Renaissance story of astuteness (cuentecillo, conseja or facecia).

I   Las harpías en Madrid

The first separate work by Castillo concerning the pranks of swindlers is *The Harpies in Madrid and the Swindlers' Coach* (*Las harpías en Madrid, y coche de las estafas*, 1631). Although this story has as its principal characters a group of female tricksters, the effective "main character" is an inanimate coach. The idea is not original; Alonso Jerónimo de Salas Barbadillo had already in 1620 thought of establishing the adventures of a coach as an element of continuity while at the same time stripping away all but the minimum of "human" biography.[2] Castillo shows us the widow Teodora and her two lovely daughters Feliciana and Luisa as they move from Seville to Madrid to improve their fortunes. On their arrival there they encounter a similar feminine group of three. A man-about-town ensnared early on in the story, Don Fernando, has a coach which he allows them all to use, and which upon his death comes into their sole possession. From this point in the novel onwards the four younger women carry out lucrative entrapments of the amorous gallants of Madrid: a Milanese, a Genoese, a priest and a fop. While each young woman carries out her deception, the others collaborate with her by assuming identities which will help to render it plausible, and the use of the coach is of course indispensable. No romantic ending is provided for this work, and it is hard to envisage one, given the dehumanized attitudes of the ladies of the coach. So Castillo closes the sequence abruptly after the last girl has effected her cheat and the whole group retires to Granada. The series of astute pranks and the "game-plans" which make them possible, form the substance of this fiction; Castillo contributes a dutiful warning after each one but these all seem superfluous. The characters are quite interchangeable, and no special talents are required of any one girl in order that she might better act the part of a *duenna*, a sister or a maid; all are capable of slipping into any role subsidiary to that of the swindler of the moment.[3] A second part is promised by Castillo (to be called *The Avengers of Swindles*), but we hear no more of this title.

II   La niña de los embustes

By 1632 Castillo must have decided that there were advantages in making the principal character of a novel of roguery a woman. So it is that we make the acquaintance of *The Girl Trickster, Teresa de Manzanares (La niña de los embustes, Teresa de Manzanares)*, the protagonist of a long, independent work of fiction. Teresa is unique among these swindlers in that she tells her own story. In this respect Castillo, in company with most novelists of his age, is not very sure of his character's capacities: it is he who informs us about what traits of character we must expect in her, and later on it is she who supplies us with comparable information—the episodes of *The Girl-Trickster* offer us, on the other hand, quite a different portrayal.

Castillo adheres to the by then consecrated method of beginning a *novela picaresca*, the backward journey to the circumstances of the protagonist's conception and simultaneous acquisition of a bad inclination. The mother of Teresa, the Galician Catalina, who lives as an orphan with her late mother's sister, the landlady of a lodging-house, is seduced by the manservant of a clergyman, who carries her off only to abandon her by the wayside. Catalina arrives in Madrid, obtains a job in a lodging-house and marries a Frenchman, Pierres. Teresa is the daughter of this marriage, but she soon becomes an orphan in her turn when Pierres drinks himself to death and Catalina dies of chagrin at being defrauded by her lover, a specialist in making political projections *(arbitrista)*. The ten-year-old Teresa finds a very adequate foster home in the house of two elderly

women who have been schooling her[4] and serves as the maid of
Teodora, the daughter of one of them. Teodora has three suitors: a
physician, a gentleman of Madrid, Don Tristán, and the student
Sarabia. Teresa already knows how to play off the affections of all
three against each of the others and secures rich presents. One
result is that the physician contrives the death of Don Tristán and
leaves Madrid in haste. It is at this time that Teresa masters the art
of wigmaking and secures a clientele of notable people, many of
them connected with the theater (something which allows Castillo
to digress into matters of a field he knows well). Sarabia appreciates
her all the more, but Teresa turns him down in favor of an old
widower, Don Lupercio. She soon becomes a widow herself after
her provocation of an incident between the old man and Sarabia.
Poor Don Lupercio dies of fright.

Teresa moves into a countess's household for two years as a maid,
but this cannot really hold her. Castillo now brings us to an episode
in her life which stands by itself. On the road to Córdoba over the
Sierra Morena she is captured by villainous bandits, but is fortunate
enough to find refuge in the simple abode of a hermit. This hermit,
in all sincerity, gives valuable information to Teresa: that he has
decided to leave the world behind after a disappointment in love.
His intended bride Leonor was compelled by her family to marry an
illegitimate scion of their own, Captain Sancho de Mendoza of
Málaga, and later fell into the hands of Moors. Leonor later died,
leaving a young daughter Feliciana in their power. When it is safe,
Teresa continues her journey to Córdoba where she resumes her
trade of wigmaking. One of her customers, Don Jerónimo, is suffering great vexation because his lady friend prefers an apparent
eunuch, the Licentiate Capadocia, to him.[5] Teresa obliges Don
Jerónimo by proposing to the eunuch that he may have hair on his
face if he is willing to employ her special unguent. The result is, of
course, that the unfortunate man is given a repellent and painful
skin disease instead, while Don Jerónimo amuses himself by forcing
him to watch the interlude *The Beard-Maker*. Teresa forthwith
leaves Córdoba for Malaga—a move which the reader will have
been anticipating ever since the hermit episode—and introduces
herself to Captain Sancho de Mendoza, becoming for a short while
Feliciana, the daughter abducted to Algiers years before. By a
stroke of ill luck the real Feliciana appears at that very time and
Teresa is shown to be an impostor. But she is among generous

people: they forgive her, and this central section of Castillo's novel comes to its conclusion.

It is time for Sarabia to reenter the story, for Teresa to marry him and join a troupe with him as a theatrical couple, though this proves to be a brief career due to the vengefulness of some humorless physicians who tire of Sarabia's stage sport at their expense. Again a widow, Teresa moves to Seville, hoping to find fortune as a false aristocrat. A gentleman returned from the Americas believes her and marries her, carrying her to his house which they are to share with his sister Leonor. The two women, in spite of the husband Don Álvar's intense jealousy, contrive to have lovers, Teresa's being a certain Don Sancho. There is an unfortunate incident when Don Sancho is called away and shuts up the two women in his room for safety. He is detained longer than he expected and asks Don Álvaro, whose matrimonial situation he is unaware of, to see that they are released. The jealous husband strikes out at his sister with a dagger, then feels such remorse that he takes his own life. At this moment Teresa suffers a reverse of fortune quite common in the careers of Castillo's characters: she can no longer pretend to nobility because someone who has reappeared out of her past life has recognized her. Once again Teresa is compelled to leave one city for another, traveling this time with a squire named Briones and two slave women, one of whom has a certain importance for the story. This is Emerenciana, who falls in with a scheme of Teresa's, and passes herself off as a niece in order to snare two *galanes*, Don Esteban and Don Leonardo.

When these two passionate young men can be appeased with promises no longer, and decide to visit the women by night, Briones saves the situation by appearing as a phantom and putting them to flight. Teresa once again presses onward to Madrid with Emerenciana, but her fortunes are from this point impossible to restore. In Madrid it happens that Don Esteban and his companion have a friend who is able to persuade Emerenciana, since she is only a slave, to rob Teresa and escape. The two false gallants reappear to cheat Teresa in their turn, and she makes her last removal, to Alcalá de Henares. It is very instructive for her that she should, in this city, encounter her childhood companion Teodora, who has been quietly and prosperously married to a tradesman all the time. Teresa's final marriage takes place, also to an honest tradesman, by whom she has children. Castillo proposes to narrate the story of one of these, a daughter, in a sequel to be called *The Congregation of Wretched-ness*. This work was never to appear.

Several notable things may be remarked of Teresa. In contrast to the other female swindlers and pranksters of Spanish fiction, and of Castillo's other works, she is a girl who knows the city before she knows the country: her native surroundings are the seething capital.[6] Very possibly for this reason she is much less concerned than the immigrant women with amassing money as an occupation. Teresa seems to prefer to scheme for social ascent, while deviating from time to time the better to carry out some heartless or even dangerous trick on one or other of Castillo's selected bearers of some stigma. She is the embodiment of restlessness, as was Madrid also its very image, and she achieves no repose.[7] It is also, it has been noted, as though she were continually attempting to run away from what she inevitably must carry with her: the fateful mark she has borne physically on her face since her birth.[8]

It is curious that Teresa should also carry from birth her bad inclination. After all, her mother Catalina is rather a sympathetic, if stupid, creature, and the other persons Castillo places among her ancestors are feckless rather than evil. Our author may conceive himself to be, however, after his fashion, more percipient: he will see a generalized inheritance of stigma, ineradicable perversity, where we would only see provincial cloddishness.[9] Castillo, in this flawed autobiography provides the disapproving epithets for his heroine's behavior while she herself insists on having many virtues we certainly do not see being practiced.[10] She is really a cynic, since unlike others among Castillo's invented company, she comes into contact with good people—whom she feels she must calumniate by attributing her own vices to them.[11] Castillo, if this is finally a moral story, must be inviting us to be cynical about Teresa.

True, she confesses to some hypocrisies,[12] and this brings us to the other interesting facet of *The Girl-Trickster*: is Teresa not then a classic "unreliable narrator"? How indeed does Castillo manage the narration of this feigned autobiography and is he aware of the pitfalls? Above all, we are always in some doubt as to when the narrative is supposed to be taking place. Teresa is not making a confession, she is merely being reminiscent, and the moral intention of the work is ultimately ignored, as we have seen.[13] It may well be—and in fact it has been suggested—that Castillo might feel he could meet all this criticism by pointing out that Teresa was after all a woman in whom impetuous action will be bound to prevail over reflection and responsibility.[14] The moment of disillusion which normally crowns a picaresque novel is entirely lacking; by and large, Teresa has learned nothing in spite of her ability to remember[15] and be knowledgeable about the inner thoughts of other people—for instance Leonardo, before she cheats him.[16] We must not, however, expect Castillo to have dominated this novelist's technique more adequate to the fictions of a later century; at least Teresa's reminiscences allowed him to impose a remarkable unity on his sequence of disparate episodes.

III   Aventuras del Bachiller Trapaza

In 1637 another novel of swindling and of more or less ingenious pranks appeared, *The Adventures of Quick-Talking Trapaza (Aventuras del Bachiller Trapaza)*, the fictional biography of Hernando Trapaza, a native of Segovia and son of Olalla Tramoya and Pedro de la Trampa (all of which names are variations on the Spanish words for "prank"). Pedro has seduced Olalla, refuses to marry her and suffers jail as a consequence. Castillo soon disposes of him by having him killed while attempting to escape. Olalla's father is concerned for the young Hernando and sees that he goes to school and later to Salamanca to study. At the university Hernando manages to acquire a small fortune as a gambler, and is later able to impose himself as a member of the gentry. He affects the name of a person of quality until, in accordance with Castillo's unfailing formula, he is recognized and denounced by an unexpected visitor from Segovia. Hernando from this point merely reverts to being a gamester and yields to his inherited inclination towards semi-criminal pranks and minor thieving, activities which bring him a certain celebrity and additionally, a female companion and criminal accomplice, Estefanía. These two insinuate themselves into the confidence of Don Lorenzo Antonio, an authentic person of quality, and then, to his intense annoyance, betray this confidence. Flight from Salamanca is the couple's only recourse. (Castillo interrupts the story here by interpolating a novella with an ancient Roman setting, told by a traveling companion).

As they approach Trujillo their carter takes on a piece of baggage for a certain Sebastián Antonio. In it there is a dead body, that of Sebastián's brother. Everyone in the cart, when concealment is impossible, is sent to jail except for Estefanía who makes straight for Sebastián's house and pretends to be the mistress of the dead man, who was killed according to her version of the events by a jealous rival. Trapaza is freed from jail in time to reunite with Estefanía, who is making off with property from her protector Sebastián's house. This reunion is, however, a brief one as after a quarrel Estefanía quits and is absent from practically all of the rest of the story, escaping with one of Trapaza's gaming companions. Trapaza continues his journey to Seville in another cart (and listens to another interpolated novella, a romance of love and tardy recognitions set in Italy).

The carter attempts to cheat, but is himself cheated by Trapaza and another passenger, Pernía. When protests are heard from the carter Trapaza decides to denounce him to the Inquisition for his profane language. Pernía proves to be a fellow of similar disposition to Trapaza's, and allows the latter to exploit gullible Andalusians by exhibiting him to them as the celebrated Nun Ensign. This is of course a reversal, since this is a matter of a man disguising himself as a woman.[17] Trapaza's incorrigible propensity for gambling away their earnings leads to their separation.

The most memorable episode of *Quick-Talking Trapaza* follows this, when Hernando becomes the servant of the eccentric Don Tomé, an *hidalgo* of by now purely imaginary economic standing. He is of course strictly comparable with other *figurones* in Castillo's dramatic works:

. . . Llegó un tal don Tomé a la conversación, con cuya venida se holgaron todos. Venía este caballero con vestido negro de gorgorán acuchillado sobre tafetán pajizo. Traía muy largas guedejas, bigotes muy levantados gracias al hierro y a la bigotera que habrían andado por allí; un sombrero muy grande, levantadas las dos faldas a la copa con unos	A certain Don Tomé showed up at this assembly, and his arrival cheered everyone up. This gentleman appeared in a black grosgrain suit, slashed with straw colored taffeta. He sported long ringlets, an upswept moustache owing much to the curling iron and the moustache trainer; a very large hat, with its brim attached to the crown by black and straw colored laces; a hatband of Italian

alamares pajizos y negros; toquilla de cintas de Italia de estos dos colores y por roseta un guante que debía ser de alguna ninfa; al cuello una banda de las mismas cintas con gran rosa atrás—cosas para calificar por figura profesa al tal sujeto.	ribbons of these same two colors, and for a rosette, a glove which surely had belonged to some wench; at his neck a scarf of the same ribbons with a great rose behind—all things which helped to mark the said individual out as a dyed-in-the-wool *figura*.

Don Tomé's status as a humorist (in the seventeenth century sense of being the character who provides the ridiculous, rather than the later meaning of the writer who records the ridiculous) is etched venomously by Castillo in the words of a servant in a gaming-house to which Tomé habitually repairs to pick up a *"barato . . . tácito socorro en paños de donativo a su pobreza"* ("a free stake . . . a silent grant-in-aid masking a donation for the relief of his poverty"). What Trapaza learns is that:

—La persona por quien me pregunta, señor galán, es un hidalgo de Andalucía, . . . Es persona de buen humor, de graciosos dichos y sazonados donaires, ... y le hacen graciosas burlas cada día, y él pasa por ellas por no perder el donativo cotidiano; . . . Esto es lo que puedo decir de don Tomé de la Plata, llamado por otro nombre de los burlones don Tomé de Rascahambre, no porque la pasa, mas porque sin renta aguarda a comer de lo que graciosamente le dan en esta casa todos los días. Pasa plaza de medio bufón	—The person you're asking me about young gentleman, is an *hidalgo* from Andalusia, . . . He is a humorist, full of merry sayings and salty jests, . . . and everyone plays amusing pranks on him day after day. He submits to them all so as not to lose his daily gratuities; . . . This is what I can tell you about Don Tomé de la Plata [i.e. "I took the money"], whom the wags have nicknamed Don Tomé Scrape-Hunger, not because he actually suffers from it, but because without any income he waits each day for what they give him to eat in this house. He indeed functions half as a buffoon . . . .

Tomé, it will be seen, combines within himself many things which Castillo always presents as ludicrous: eccentric style of speech and gesture, *hidalgo* (genteel) pretensions, curious costume, courtly love in an unworthy vessel and, of course, that obscene filament connecting all of these, poverty. Yet this ridiculous personage believes himself to be the lover of, (and to have his love returned by) the most noble lady Doña Brianda. When Tomé and Trapaza are invited to the country house of Doña Brianda's father, a trap is laid for this *figurón*, and Trapaza is disloyal enough to cooperate with the heartless aristocrats. Again it is the trick of the feigned phantom of the restless dead.

A doctor and his much older wife accept Trapaza, who is once again penniless, into their house as a servingman, but he cannot resist making out-of-place jests about his ill-assorted employers and is obliged to leave.[18] There is a reunion with his old confederate Pernía, but this is the point in the story at which Trapaza passes through a curious phase. He actually begins to feel a genuine passion for the highborn Serafina, whom he first learned to admire in a painted likeness. As though by the occult force of platonic love, Trapaza adapts himself incredibly well to the role of gentle lover, inventing a suitably magnanimous past to accord with it. Really however, another side of Trapaza is trying to get hold of Serafina's dowry, and again Castillo rushes to the aid of a person of quality menaced by the sharper or *buscón*, producing of course a personage from Trapaza's less chivalrous years gone by.

Trapaza moves on to Madrid, again enriches himself at the gaming tables, and importunes high society under the guise of a Portuguese nobleman. At this point close to the novel's end he rediscovers Estefanía, now a widow, and leaves her expecting a child by him. Another possibility of marriage presents itself to Trapaza, but Estefanía denounces him and he becomes fully a *pícaro* at last, if only in conforming to the model of Guzmán de Alfarache in that both characters end by being sentenced to the galleys.

Castillo, it will be at once observed, deals much more harshly with the male protagonist or anti-hero of this first novel of fraud written in the third person. There is definitely a greater emphasis laid upon the issue of social ambition, and there are some tense moments when it seems that the charmed world of gentlefolk is to be invaded by the upstart bastard, Trapaza. No doubt we have here Castillo's reason for his harshness. The story has a sequel in *The*

She-Stoat of Seville, Fishhook of the Purses of Others (*La garduña de Sevilla, anzuelo de las bolsas*, 1642), the third-person narrative of the life of Rufina, daughter of the ex-galley-slave Trapaza and the now remorseful Estefanía.[19] This work moves us into an atmosphere of more reprehensible criminality than was found in any of the previous stories. Once more there is an alternation of swindling—or plain robbery—and practical joking.

IV La garduña de Sevilla

Rufina is already five years of age when her parents marry; she was of course the child begotten in Madrid. But Castillo seems to prefer that his protagonists shall be orphans as soon as practicable. Estefanía is the first to die, and then Trapaza himself loses his life defending the honor of Rufina against her despicable rogue of a lover, Roberto. She has while very young indeed been married off to Lorenzo, an older man with the (for Castillo) unpardonable vice of parsimony. Roberto does not live to enjoy adultery with Rufina, since another of her admirers, Feliciano, murders him when he returns to Seville. All this inconstancy is too much for Lorenzo who dies of a broken heart. Rufina, now free, turns to a criminal life with a professional thief Garay. Their first victim is the miser Marquina, whom Rufina manages to fascinate and later persuade that he is responsible for another man's death. Marquina hides his wealth and flees, making it an easy haul for Rufina and Garay. On the journey which they undertake towards Madrid they listen to a novella told them by a priest.

The criminal pair for once attempt to give assistance to a dying man out of pity, and are arrested as his possible attackers. Happily, they can prove this is not so and both of them find a helper in another miser, the Genoese Feluchi, in Córdoba. Garay manages to swindle him by means of a pretended knowledge of alchemy, and the two move off towards Málaga. While they pass the night in a wood by the roadside they overhear three other thieves, one of whom is the false hermit Crispín, discuss their robberies. At the next inn Rufina and Garay are able to administer a sleeping draught to Crispín and make off with what he has stolen. At this point in the story another interpolated novella is offered, not very appropriately, by one of Crispín's confederates who is by no means courtly or of gentle soul.

Once the pair of scoundrels have reached Madrid again, Crispín
soon locates them, posing though they are as Doña Emerenciana
and her father Don Jerónimo, but Crispín makes the mistake of not
taking immediate revenge himself. An accomplice named Jaime
who is expected to do this falls in love with Rufina instead. This love
is, incredibly, shared by Rufina and, again incredibly, the ruffian
Jaime undertakes the telling of the third of Castillo's interpolated
novellas of love and constancy.[20] Together the lovers rob Crispín
and send him to his death on the gallows, while Garay goes despite
his advanced age to row in the galleys. Rufina and her Jaime effect a
final robbery at the expense of a theatrical entrepreneur, and escape
to Saragossa. Jaime, surviving Rufina's other two male accomplices,
actually marries her before this escape—to freedom; not to any
punishment. Castillo promises once again a sequel, which apparently allows him to pass off his story as a moral one: the missing
retribution is presumably to be anticipated in that sequel.
But . . . Jaime is of Rufina's own class.[21]
    The character Rufina dominates this novel. All but an insignificant
few are either her accomplices or her dupes, and occasionally one of
the former will pass over into the latter group as Castillo allows the
she-stoat's good looks and "femininity" to play a role in the general
criminal confusion. All of Rufina's male confederates, Garay, Crispín and Jaime, are held by sexual or vindictive emotional tension.
The novel—once one separates out the interpolations, which are
especially bulky in this work[22]—concerns the ways in which Rufina,
once she arrives at adulthood, seizes the opportunities provided by
accidental slackenings in that tension.

V   Castillo's Characterization

    What strikes us when we consider Castillo's novels of swindling or
ingenious trickery is the absence, or at least the totally static presence, of the upper classes in the array of characters. For this reason
we might characterize these works as fictions in which the parasitic
gentlemen's companions—such as those in the comedies—have
come to the foreground. Additionally, given Castillo's preferred deviation from the conventional, they have become feminized. The
origins of the crooks of either sex are emphatically lower class, and
this accounts, without further explanation, for their bad inclinations.
Rufina's Jaime for instance, is presented as an honest provincial to

begin with, but one whose ambitions have led him into the villainies
of the city. It is presented as only logical that when a character, say
Teresa, rises in the social scale, that character will be tempted into
worse behavior. Castillo does not moralize about this irrational perception, but merely presents it for our amusement as yet another
cliché adhering to his chosen form.[23]

The male swindlers are the more attractive characters in the long
run. Domingo ("The Proteus of Madrid") has the virtue, in his
creator's eyes, of not seeking acceptance among the gentry; he
merely cheats amusingly for a living until a sentence to row in the
galleys puts a stop to it. Hernando Trapaza, who is in some ways his
more protracted version as a character, goes through many phases in
the course of the two novels he appears in, his almost heroic status
at the end atoning after a fashion for the bad start he had made long
before in seeking to insinuate himself among those of a socially
higher rank. What slowly transforms him is apparently the occult
effect of his loyalty: first to masters and companions, although he has
no special vocation to the life of a servant, and secondly to his
paramour Estefanía. Even when she deserts him he already grieves
for her absence rather than for the money she has escaped with. He
goes to the galleys moreover, not for his swindling nor for the debts
his vice of gambling has brought upon him, but for love of her.
Finally he dies in a duel defending the honor of their unworthy
daughter.[24]

None of the women characters of any importance in these novels
of Castillo's is so admirable. The "harpies of Madrid" are difficult to
account for in realistic terms; perhaps they ought to be called en-
trepreneurs, since they have a quenchless rapacity without any of
the lasciviousness which might enmesh them in prostitution of any
description. Their overriding talent is for ridicule, and that for its
own sake given that the gleanings are so relatively small. Teresa, the
"girl-trickster" is more an example of the humble maiden perverted,
quite different from the harpies in her ambition to rise in the world.
An industrious artisan at the outset, she marries but falls into a
liaison. On her husband's death she feels apparent remorse and
dismisses her lover; Castillo then, may be representing her as pos-
sessed of a certain virtue. A moral decline ensues when her second
husband insists that she take lovers, and yet a third stage of baseness
is to come when, after her third marriage, she defrauds an heiress of
her valuables. Teresa suffers in no way at society's hands at the close

of her story, unless according to Castillo's curious idea of retribution she has gained sufficient punishment in acquiring a detested merchant as a husband and a certain chagrin at seeing the placid Teodora, who has arrived at the same point after a life of no comparable hazards or villainies. Castillo, as we have seen, ends by promising a sequel so that we cannot judge whether the trajectory of baseness will resume or whether Teresa intends to reform for good.

The "she-stoat" Rufina is greedy and without compassion of any kind from the beginning, and she gravitates towards bad company as her natural element. The only mitigation of this perception of her is to point out that her adversaries, misers and the like, are more or less equally repellent; we may find ourselves tempering our indignation at her misdeeds accordingly. Robbery and delation are part of her inclination, though Castillo allows her the vestigial feminine propensity for falling in love when a suitable final episode arrives. To describe the female tricksters in all three novels—Estefanía holds to a moral position conveniently midway between Teresa's and Rufina's—is to imply that Castillo has limned them in lurid or dark colors, but this is never noticeable on account of the unfailing series of scenes of witty humiliation of others which they all engage in, sometimes even to the detriment of their swindling careers and seldom for any tangible monetary gain.

This might be a convenient juncture at which to pose the question of how feminine—how "feministic"—are these *busconas* or female rogues. The question is incidentally bound up with that of the possibly superior femininity of the first-person presentation of Teresa over that of the other two third-person presentations. The customary intrusiveness of the author Castillo—and nothing else could be expected in his period—turns this promising distinction into a mirage: Teresa can utter a phrase like *"admirándome de cuan estragada elección tenemos las mujeres"* ("astonished as I was at the vitiated choices we women make") in no spirit of irony. Yet she and the others are indeed created differently from the male *pícaros;* they are not just accidentally clothed as women. Part of the difference, leaving a shared "bad inclination" aside, is that which lies between intelligence and astuteness, attributed to male and female swindlers respectively. Proceeding from this convenient axiom, Castillo as a writer of works of entertainment is bound to prefer astuteness as more absorbing and amusing for his readers.[25] Beyond that, the quotient of femininity in the works goes little beyond the delineation of even a free woman's limited life in which her "vitiated choices" impel her either towards frivolity or a *galanterie* which is its own justification.[26]

As we have noticed, Castillo did not invent the female rogue. Her origins are no doubt medieval, but long after the Middle Ages misogyny was in the ascendant. *Busconas* peep into the story of *Lazarillo de Tormes* already in the decade after 1550. They dominate certain chapters of Mateo Alemán's *Guzmán de Alfarache* (1599; 1605), notably when the hero is robbed by one of the elegant women of Saragossa as he fondles her.[27] Later, from occupying only individual chapters, the *buscona* (female rogue) advances to take over entire works, the most striking of which is *La ingeniosa Elena, hija de Celestina (The Crafty Elena, Daughter of Celestina)* by Salas Barbadillo (1612). This is a prostitute's biography but Salas has pruned away the misogynistic platitudes of former writers and allows Elena to reflect on her actions and on her unpropitious ancestry and upbringing. No special knowledge of the feminine soul on Salas's part is to be inferred, the author's voice echoing consistently the voice of social order.[28] Elena is finally sentenced and put to death, something that elsewhere never happens in the picaresque fictions of the age. It is very revealing that the author decides that the punishment embodies a caution against conduct that men should abhor when they see it, not that women ought not to imitate. Without a doubt their "vitiated choices" when no man governs their wills would, in Salas's view, render them impervious to the lesson of Elena. We could also conclude that some writers chose the female criminal as their subject because she is more sensational to read about.[29]

Of course, it is true that a more independent woman will on occasion abandon the traditionally feminine incentives and pursuits and become a criminal. Rufina never intends to work with her hands as Teresa does fairly constantly; hence Rufina has more freedom and the propensity towards criminal living.[30] One of Castillo's resolutions is marriage, at least at the end of a story: Teresa and Rufina do this, and Estefanía does likewise early in a sequel. If the beginning of each novel shows the poisoning, in one way or another, of human relationships, at the end marriage is the antidote. Between these extremes of each novel, however, there are many chapters in which the perverse *buscona* acts with complete freedom.[31]

These swindlers are impossible to understand in isolation from

their dupes; when the former group indulges for a moment in a rest
from its ambitions of rising in the social scale it is usually engaged in
preying upon, cheating and "punishing"—apparently with Castillo's
own approval—a very special set of people within society: not the
upper classes who are shown to be invulnerable to the swindlers,
but the eccentrics and monomaniacs, those who more or less ludicrously do not conform.[32] Even those who, in obedience to tradition, respect unreflectingly the man of law and the man of religion
are surprisingly enough grouped with these gullible eccentrics.[33]
Castillo is therefore apparently prompting his readers to despise
these victims, while advantage is being taken at the same time of the
moral holiday his stories afford. But there is more to it than this. A
little beneath the surface of the narration of the often hideous pranks
played and cheats effected we can discern another reason for the
plight of the dupes: their position in the social scale of wealth. Each
of the ridiculous figures—and especially those forced through poverty to live in the country—each poetaster and ungainly lover could,
in the event of his having more money, have avoided the attentions of
these cheats and mockers.[34] And as a corollary, if these cheats had
really been interested in duping people for substantial gain, Castillo
might have shown them in pursuit of better quarry, with a better
return in hand for the time and ingenuity they expend—or for the
effort expended, in the case of the women characters, in keeping
themselves beautiful, young and witty. To inquire why Castillo's
puppets do not do this is as fruitless as to ask why some of his
characters, once they have acquired considerable legacies, promptly
lose them.

All this does not disqualify Castillo's novels of ingenious fraud
from being vigorous and attractive works of fiction. The relentless
onslaught of impish tricksters on ridiculous or lustful victims sounds
like a prescription for monotony of plot, helped out by outrageous
coincidences and strokes of fortune reminiscent of the tired-out
Byzantine romance.[35] This leaves aside, however, the never failing
movement, as though for its own sake, of the endlessly resourceful
characters amid an interesting array of minor figures of the type we
have already met in interludes and plays. Each of these has his own
curious characteristics and manner of expressing himself: a carter
(*Quick-Talking Trapaza*), a Basque ("The Proteus of Madrid"), a
political projector (*The Girl-Trickster*) and a "wholesome" holy
hermit (also in *The Girl-Trickster*), among a number of others.

CHAPTER 5

Novellas of Romance and Fortune

BETWEEN 1625 and 1649 Castillo Solórzano produced fifty-five novellas concerning young personages engaged in hazards of love and fortune, together with two longer books which represent conglomerations of identical material (*Lisardo enamorado; Los amantes andaluces*). It has been observed that they fall neatly into two categories:[1] (a) a novella "of manners," set in Spain and involving wellborn young men and women, characters "of quality," in perils and misunderstandings invariably connected with love; (b) a novella "of fantasy," in which the characters are kings and princes, shown against settings outside Spain and perhaps in a more or less remote antiquity. Their themes are of heroism rather than of the chances of love, and it is in these novellas that Castillo will be found most often to moralize, as though they were demonstrations of virtuous conduct for the instruction of princes, and as such a very tardy vestige of a medieval literary genre. In this second group there will be discovered of course, the abundant anachronisms which few popular novelists are able to avoid.

In Castillo's novellas, plots are everything, and there are two primary observations to be made about these. First, they stand in a direct line of succession to the Spanish translation (by Fernando de Mena, 1587) of Heliodorus's *Aethiopic Romance,* a Greek fiction of the early period of the Byzantine Empire and second, their recurrent situations are absolutely comparable to what we encounter in the Spanish *comedia* of the period, after the universal innovations made in it by Lope de Vega. The name *novella comediesca* has even been proposed for the type.[2] Interchanges of material were possible between the two forms, and we have the notable example here of *Outrage Atoned For.* Castillo himself was inclined to attribute his choice of novella presentation to the difficulty of attracting the attentions of theatrical producers *(autores)* to his dramatic talents, refer-

63

ring in those days to the hegemony of Lope de Vega on the Madrid stage. *Galanes* and *damas* also constitute the *dramatis personae* of the *comedia;* all that Castillo, in the instance we have mentioned, had to do was to supply his own novella with a *gracioso* or fun maker and a corresponding female role, that of lady's maid and subsequent object of the *gracioso's* more or less loutish attentions.

Heliodorus's tale, given immense prestige as a prose equivalent of literary epic by turn-of-the-century theorists like Alonso López, *el Pinciano*, is essentially that of two lovers "of quality" who, by unusual accidents of fate, are separated from parents, fatherlands and eventually each other. In the course of the book all kinds of perils and disappointments come their way, but they are perils and disappointments which the "virile" tenacity of the heroine and the invincible chastity of both heroine and hero are able to overcome. We encounter in the *Aethiopic Romance* a set of interwoven stories, autobiographies of minor characters and the like, quite comparable in tenor to the main story. To point out that there are curious descriptions of cities and sanctuaries, an account of the repellent ritual of a sorceress and finally, a lovers' meeting and a family recognition after pages of suspense, is surely to remind the modern reader of a host of novels of love and adventure which he or she will have read. Heliodorus's story, since it was discovered at a moment in history when spreading literacy coincided with a new restlessness in the European soul, truly is the wellspring of much modern fiction; not, however, of many masterpieces. It may be remarked at this point that Castillo's reluctance to exclude moralizing set-pieces from even short novellas (for instance in "Guardian to His Own Son" ["El ayo de su hijo"]) is probably an aspect of his close dependence on his model Heliodorus.[3]

The plots of Castillo's novellas were, as we have noticed, interchangeable with those of many three-act *comedias* of the day, and portions of such plots might also be displaced from play to play, story to story or play to story. This is because the whole of literature was then to a high degree theatrical; the authors cast themselves more as dramatic producers with no compunction about speaking out as such, than as self-effacing, however "omniscient" narrators of events. Hardly anything in Castillo comes out from a character's point of view, and in this lies the contrast between him and the greater works of Cervantes.[4] It has been said that for Castillo the novella was a handy receptacle.[5] Even his most rapidly-moving actions adhere, in respect of their invention, to current theatrical practice. There is, for instance, a tripartite structure which corresponds exactly to the dramatic model. Florence Yudin has detected the three stages of the typical plot: (a) the exposition and the delineation of the characters' motives; (b) the *enredo* or baffling complication: all the obstacles and isolation besetting *galán* and *dama;* (c) the *desenlace* or resolution attendant upon the inevitable turn in their fortunes. A love affair is not a thing suffered internally, but is also constructed by Castillo to be "acted out";[6] it is delineated as exteriorized action and also has its three stages: (a) the initial scene of arousal of passion, its absorption into an ocean of *discreteo* (dialogue about love and constancy, with a high redundancy factor and dependent on the repetition of words and phrases derived ultimately from the troubadours, the late-medieval song-collections and the more recent Italian theorists of platonic love [Leo the Hebrew, Marius Equicola and others, whom Castillo would not necessarily need to have read in the text]); (b) the seduction, followed by separations and moments of despair; (c) the bliss of reunion and the reward of sorely tried constancy to continue forever and ever.[7]

The greater number of Castillo's novellas are comprised within nine "frame-stories." This is the familiar device first authorized by Boccaccio three centuries earlier in his *Decameron.* Castillo, however, never imitates the ancient master in conceiving of anything so horrible as a plague in the city as a pretext for assembling people of noble natures in pleasant surroundings. The cheerfulness of the country seats in his frame-stories is emphasized; even the convalescent Casandra is no longer feeling too ill *(To Cheer Up Casandra)* and besides, her palace is sumptuous and full of luxurious features which Castillo describes enthusiastically. This pervasive wholesomeness of the surroundings connects with the stories contained within the narrative frames, that is, the stories told by the personages in them: we feel that no emotional shock or moral dilemma will ever be able to break in upon the wholesome characters assembled there in any particularly alarming manner.[8] Obviously, in terms of the history of fictional techniques, Castillo is much less sophisticated than Cervantes, who had, as far back as 1613, dispensed with the frame-story in his *Novelas ejemplares (Exemplary Novels).* We are as it were transported back to the world of Castiglione's *Courtier* (1528), in which the telling of stories is recommended, among other social accomplishments, as an instrument for heightening the tone of a gathering or of a court.

Another influence upon Castillo's choice of the frame-story convention may well be his day-to-day experience of literary societies, actually another part of Castiglione's legacy to European culture. In these meetings narrative themes and moral disquisitions of an abstract type were proposed, formulated and judged. The five gentlemen of *The Plain of Valencia* (*Huerta de Valencia*, 1629) do in fact in a rural setting simulate just such a gathering, each one of them proposing to his companions a poetic theme which he must indite, and each one of them telling a story.[9] Not all of Castillo's formulas for the frame situation are alike, however: *Merry Days* (*Jornadas alegres*, 1626) allows for a leisurely trip from Talavera to Madrid by a company of gentlefolk who have acquired a professional entertainer, while *Entertaining Evenings* (*Tardes entretenidas*, 1625) introduces us to two widows with their two daughters who are all taking the waters at a resort near Madrid. *Nights of Pleasure* (*Noches de placer*, 1631) and *Time of Rejoicing* (*Tiempo de regocijo*, 1627) permit Castillo to exploit a reference to the custom of celebrating family reunions at religious festivals year by year. He follows Tirso de Molina, whose *Cigarrales de Toledo* (*Country Seats Near Toledo*, 1624) had, however, immediate novelistic intrigue directly built into the frame-story, so that his characters were active pursuers of adventure and passion instead of mere listeners to narratives of romance in the lives of others. Frame-stories of whatever form are, of course, excellent receptacles for observations on moral philosophy and other abstract topics. As stories became shorter the little essays, which long romances in the wake of the *Aethiopic Romance* traditionally contained perforce, had to find a habitation somewhere else; the frame-story was the perfect location. Apparently the borderline, so unmistakable to us today, between novella and moral essay was quite imperceptible in Castillo's day.[10] This certainly allowed every writer of fiction to stuff his productions with an adventitious "profundity," and no doubt allowed many a reader to assure himself that here was a royal road to moral sagacity.

When we come to the characters found in Castillo's fiction of this type a difficulty arises. It is extremely hard to describe them apart from the moral atmosphere they have their being in, since they are so little more than embodiments of the omnipresent prejudices of an author of "purveyed literature," engaged in his task of assembling and giving a new surface to the well tried structures of romance. There are discrepancies in the invention of characters between those novellas set in Spain and those the plots of which develop in places far away in space or time, notably in that women characters in the latter type of story may be, in their quality of queens or princesses, free agents in securing their destinies. Absent in all the stories, however, are all considerations of "psychology"[11] or even the emotional suspense which gave, in its time, a certain vivacity to the ancestral *Aethiopic Romance* of Heliodorus. The mainspring of virtually every novella is some aspect of the notion of rivalry: between brothers (for love or family esteem); between one amorous princess with a taste for music and *discreteo* and another with an amazonian taste for power; between a gallant with all the best qualities—not excluding that of noble poverty[12]—and another less perfect young man who has the lady's family on his side. The rival in any of these cases need not actually exist in the story; enough tension will exist even then to instil compassion, or at least partisanship and curiosity into the minds of the intended readers.[13] Any minor characters who appear in these novellas will have even more evidences of the ready-made in their makeup; irrational behavior and stylized tics of speech practically exhaust their characterization. If they are servants, jailers or lawyers there is every chance that they will be dishonest and venal. Finally, that special sentimental figure, the hermit, will be depended upon to bring in an appeal to callow religiosity.[14] When love has been scorned there is little remedy for a gallant but the hermitage, if we exclude the duel. Such are the clichés of the novella of love and fortune that a lowly-born swindler like Castillo's Trapaza, in his novel of that name, can master them and pass himself off credibly as a passionate gallant.

The moral picture reflected in Castillo's novellas of this type is the usual one in his epoch: perforce the novelist must present exceptional happenings, while at the same time there must be a reinforcement of a very unexceptional scheme of values. Only a relative escape from this dilemma—which Castillo would, of course, not consider such—is provided by the choice of setting we have referred to on a previous page, either in Spain (novella "of manners") or in some other place and time (novella "of fantasy"). In the novellas of this latter type the moral scene is involved with affairs of state, often conducted by great ladies of the blood royal: wars, diplomacy, questions of succession and the visual pageantry of state. Monarchs in these stories, it being another country and period, may earn punishment for misdeeds and go through with marriages to humbler partners. Deviation from acceptable "Spanish" behavior appears;

Octavio ("Ingratitude and its Punishment," in *Nights of Pleasure*) is an Italian who refuses to honor his word to Casandra. Her avenger is willing to marry her even though she bears Octavio's child. But this instance implies that erotic interest is prevalent in the group set abroad; the more obvious outcome of most of the stories is a scene of reparation for calumny, injustice or sheer ill luck, any one of which will have driven a prince into disguise or self-expatriation.

There is a curious case of the intersection of the two categories of novella in "The Spanish Innate Quality" ("La inclinación española"), where a Spanish gentleman in Italy shows an untutored mastery of swordsmanship against formidable partners. This chauvinistic detail is a good introduction to the very different moral scene of the novellas "of manners." In this instance, as we have observed, the characters populating the novellas are similar in social position and temperament to those listening to the story in the frame narratives: that is, they are Spanish and of the middling nobility. The special phenomena contained in the plots of these novellas "of manners" have been examined in the chapter on Castillo's plays. In résumé we need only insist on the curious restriction of the lives of both heroes and ladies to the pursuit of pleasure, until this is interrupted by the amorous crisis and its sequels: rivalries, *empleos* (the usual term signifying the deflection of a passion towards another object)[15] and misunderstandings. When the lovers' distress is resolved, the pursuit of pleasure can resume. The triumph of the most conventional social opinion must be assured, and here the universal solvent— bearing away all vestiges of grief and shame—is affluence and the possibility of ostentation. There is some moral criticism, though it is by no means incisive: the diatribes against the use of cosmetics, arrogance, avarice and even jealousy seem to be animated by an all-embracing compunction where the danger of the hero's appearing to slide downwards, onto a moral plane thought more typical of the unrefined mass, might flash across the reader's mind.[16]

CHAPTER 6

Castillo in Spanish and European Literature

I *The Traditions Behind Castillo's Works*

CASTILLO, in his introduction to *Entertaining Evenings*, assures us that his works are entirely original:

. . . lo que te puedo asegurar es que ninguna cosa de las que en este libro te presento es traducción italiana, sino todas hijas de mi entendimiento; que me corriera mucho de oír de mí lo que de los que traducen, o trasladan por hablar con más propiedad. . . .	What I can assure you is that nothing of what is contained in this book I present you with is translated from Italian. Everything is the offspring of my own mind, and I should be very ashamed to hear said of me what is said of the others who do translate or, more accurately, transpose.

As the texts of his novellas stand, this is certainly true. The conception he has of a novella plot, however, and the devices he is aware of for making the reader keep his attention on the fable, owe everything to the discoveries of the Italian *novellieri*. Cervantes had made a very similar claim in the prologue to his *Exemplary Novels* in 1613, but with more justification. The novellas by Cervantes which are always singled out for admiration, and (in some estimations) even some of those which are customarily neglected, have a new profundity in their conception: real human passions are studied, and the loose ends of which every life consists are ingeniously suggested and reassembled by a disenchanted but highly individual mind. From this master Castillo appears to have learned nothing at all. Where Cervantes, in his most admirable and permanent pieces, chose to

69

delineate the planless, the exceptional and the enigmatic, Castillo chose to look for the rigid scheme into which to mould the narrative plasma. This was, as we have noticed, a scheme corresponding to that of the three-act *comedia* of the type formulated by Lope de Vega. If we needed to look for a representative predecessor in the world of the Spanish novella, we should probably find him in Juan Timoneda, author of a *Book of Tales* (*Patrañuelo*, 1567) and an ingenious adapter of Italian literary genres into Spanish. Timoneda's twenty-two stories—of which some ten are of romance and fortune—are usually pure derivations from the well known collections of *novelle* in Italy, and occasionally, for instance in "Patraña XXI" ("The Pilgrimage of Geroncia"), they are unified stories forged by Timoneda from disparate pre-existing Italian sources. He is, however, an unmistakable *naïf* among story writers, though he knows how to hold one's attention and space out his material. Castillo was to avail himself of entirely comparable matters for development into stories, but brought into evidence a new sophistication in diction, in ability to organize it all into the characteristic three-moment pattern—and to cover his tracks in the matter of his borrowings!

Between 1567 and 1625, the date of Castillo's first collection of novellas, there had evolved in Spain a whole tradition of prose fiction on an ampler scale. Timoneda himself, in his longest piece, "Patraña XI" ("Apolonio, Prince of Tyre") had stood on the threshold of this new domain. This was the genre of story often typified as the "Byzantine novel" (since its prototypes were later found to date from the years of the later Roman Empire, and to hail from the urbanized Greek speaking provinces). In Spain, as we saw in the previous chapter, there was enthusiastic reading of the principal "Byzantine" romance, Heliodorus's *Aethiopic Romance* (sometimes called after its two chief characters, *Theagenes and Chariclea*). Many Spanish imitations of this work, close to the turn of the century, are strongly marked by its atmosphere of restless pilgrimage frequently alternating as a theme with the anguish of captivity. Both pilgrimage and captivity are adequate to suggest a metaphysical distress afflicting lovers separated by continual misfortunes. Novels of this kind, produced by Cervantes, Gonzalo de Céspedes or Lope de Vega, had a capacity for absorbing into their desultory plots a great deal of extraneous matter. Indeed there existed the powerful warrant of the *Aethiopic Romance* also for this. Castillo then, stood heir to the weaknesses as well as the strengths of this romance tradition as he adopted the miscellany pattern from Diego Rosel y Fuenllana's *Applications and Transformations* (*Aplicaciones y transformaciones*, 1613), Alonso Jerónimo de Salas Barbadillo's *The House of Irreproachable Pleasure* (*La casa del placer honesto*, 1620) and Tirso de Molina's *The Country-Houses near Toledo* (*Los Cigarrales de Toledo*, 1621).

Fictions concerning the pilgrimage of love and virtue lend themselves to counterfeiting on the level of the everyday and even the scurrilous. This is, of course, a not unimportant reason why we have Cervantes's *Don Quijote,* but the kind of work which brings down those high ascetic romances to the plane of "realism" in the experience of Castillo seems to have been more of the order of Alonso Fernández de Avellaneda's spurious continuation of *Don Quijote* (1614), or Salas Barbadillo's *Pedro de Urdemalas* (1620) and *The Resourceful Elena* (*La ingeniosa Elena*, 1612), and of Juan Cortés de Tolosa's *Lazarillo de Manzanares* (1625). Although some of these novels may be longer than Castillo's novels of swindling, from them he certainly derived his memorable characters Domingo, Trapaza, Teresa de Manzanares and Rufina. Salas Barbadillo in fact seems to have prompted him to choose the female swindler as major character; Castillo was not therefore even original in this. The general idea of Castillo as a continuer of the Spanish fictional tradition is then, one of a man who derived everything from books and from frequent conversation in academies with their authors. Only in one instance would we care to venture the assertion that he has sought and found a motive in the unwritten folklore of his native northwestern Spain, and this is the story-within-a-story of underwater adventure in "El conde de las legumbres."[1]

II *The Literary Impact of Castillo*

The reputation of our author stood in the literary societies of his day and stands today, primarily on his ability to create *figuras del donaire* (figures who provoke merriment, or who have it as their element) and a special language of equivocation with which to surround them. It is notoriously difficult to plot the precise course of the inception of all this matter into Spain, but both figures and poetic equivocations must certainly have entered from Italy and from her literary societies of earlier date. The implications for both the development of the *figurón* or buffoon, and the swallowing-up of the human figure in a torrent of dehumanizing linguistic play, of the sensational theories about human and animal physiognomy published by the Neapolitan Giambattista Della Porta, cannot be neglected as extra-literary determinants of the preferences of Castillo's public.[2] We may contrast Castillo's *entremeses* with those of that greater man of letters Francisco de Quevedo. Amid all the farcical cruelty and the mockery of the irremediably human in Quevedo's interludes we catch a note of serious moral consideration about marital fidelity, or about the primordial awesomeness of the moment of childbirth—while Castillo on the other hand chooses to remain (and no doubt he does it with the complicity of a whole generation)—on a plane of persiflage aimed at the "imposture" of poor devils like the chestnut vendor.

III   *Purveyed Literature*

The discussion of Castillo's fiction in the preceding pages will no doubt, have induced a feeling of familiarity in the reader of our day. The schemes which underlie the novella and the plays bear a distinct resemblance to those of many durable forms of narrative down to our own times: the tale of adventure, the sentimental romance of lovers, and the "thrilling" story of coincidences and the supernatural. To call this type of fiction popular literature would be, however, erroneous, due to the manner in which an acquaintance with it is actually obtained by its readers.[3] This is more accurately *purveyed literature*, acquired in the same way as any other commodity to be consumed and affording in the same way the satisfactions asked of it. Primarily it is a sub-literature which invites the reader to a simple, "healthy" world where the complexities as well as the aridities of life have been removed.[4] In all ages this type of book has invited the reader to identify intensely, as much through adventitious references to clothing, to sexual habits or to characters with a privileged status, as through a predictably satisfying solution to the plot.[5] Beyond this appeal to identification its author will have made no attempt at conveying a problematical reality.[6]

Novels which are comprised in this ancient tradition of purveyed fiction—and here Castillo's productions will henceforward be included—made their appeal to their readers' desires for wishes to be fulfilled, identified as these are with the wishes of the personages in the stories. This is another way of saying that their authors have provided such works with structures of consciousness and motivation never more than commensurable with those of the readers'. These patterns of illusion are, it will be pointed out, also discoverable in "higher" fiction, but there inevitably they are mitigated by disillusioning ingredients: irony, tragic potentialities, problems beyond solution, and a system of rewards and punishments distributed haphazardly.[7]

The characteristics of Castillo's fictions viewed from this standpoint are best determined by observing the fortunes of the characters "of quality": the *galán* (young hero) and the *dama* (sentimental heroine). It is the presence of these two which endows Castillo's stories—and plays—with their durable "romantic" surface and which reveals also their ideological underpinning. It is their absence from the novels of swindling, as we have suggested, which accounts for the special anarchical and venal tone we encounter in them.

These young persons of quality are primarily social, not sentimental creatures. Their adventures are adventures within the pyramid of society and their loves are social attachments. Money and what money buys, notably opportunities for ostentation, assume a remarkable importance in the stories and the plays. Having money solves so many things, and is even capable of canceling out sorrow. The lack of it leads to shame; men of noble origin are forced by impecuniousness to retire to the country.[8] Conversely the city and the nearby garden-begirt estate exist in the stories as theaters for ostentation almost exclusively. Castillo's eulogies of such resorts are typical of all purveyed fiction: they supply no real information about the settings of stories, but rather incite reminiscence, or a vague longing to be included in the scenery, in the reader. So many cities mentioned by Castillo are spoken of merely in terms of their principal promenades.[9]

The unenlightened attitudes with respect to money do not, of course, correspond to anything outside books in Castillo's time. A plebeian in the novels cannot acquire gentility, while a personage of quality cannot penetrate the barrier above him or her: that of *la sangre* (inherited nobility of great antiquity).[10] If this mythical impermeability of classes ever had a semblance of existence it had certainly been superseded by Castillo's time. Like the perennial writer of purveyed fiction however, he is obliged to present this state of affairs, as natural and immutable.[11] Historically we hear of no protest about the arrival of the rich on the part of more venerable aristocrats.

The panorama of moral judgments is all of a piece with this. The vices which Castillo singles out to condemn are either related to *miseria* (parsimony) or *soberbia* (egoism). Generosity, charitableness and friendship in need are eulogized, particularly since they concord with economic prudence without impairing the hero's chances of ostentation.[12] Pride is anathematized because it may subvert the person of quality into antisocial failings such as ingratitude, ambition or treachery. It follows that these will be the vices which beset the rivals of the hero in many stories, whether there is a social or psychological reason for them or not. The heroes on the other hand, will just as often have the virtues, though they will not have any conspicuous common sense.[13] Success in love, or what passes for it in these deformed fictional worlds will be the most evident sign and guerdon of possessing the virtues mentioned. The heroines' set of virtues is even more predictable and unlifelike: all they require is an ability to insist most shrilly on modesty in visible relationships, a tenacity in securing promises of marriage and a certain vindictiveness. In this highly social world all seductions are put right by marriages, murders may be momentary inconveniences, but practical jokes and foolish sentimental experimentation can be thought of as enough to occupy a young woman's waking hours.

The same socialization of the fiction prevents the novels of swindling from being satirical.[14] More classes of society are studied, but always superciliously, as though the reader of quality—and his more numerous sympathizers—wished to look into the circumstances of poor *hidalgos*, artisans, servants and peasants as into a pond full of humble organisms. No doubt such a reader was capable of feeling an inexplicable menace at the thought of the erosion of some—hardly, to us, significant—class barriers as rogues and tarts promoted themselves, but all is really well: the persons of quality are effectively absent from the scenes of their parasites' momentary triumphs.[15]

We have frequently implied that Castillo's fictions, in prose and in dramatic form, constitute a kind of milestone in the progress of purveyed literature. What examples have we of earlier manifestations of this commodity? Probably the earliest works identifiable as having their place here are the romances of the Middle Ages on the subject of Troy,[16] the humbler texts out of which Boccaccio,

Chaucer and Henryson wrought more respectable works of art. But the moment of early plentitude for such romances arrived with the wider dissemination of the printed book. *Amadís de Gaula (Amadis of Gaul)* acquired its first readership among the noble and wealthy, there can be no doubt of that, and spread among them and their socially ascendant sympathizers also a taste for ornate diction and affected melancholy in stories above love, friendship, honor and danger—a diction and a melancholy to be exhibited in prolix letters and conversations throughout the subsequent series of chivalresque works by the talented and untalented. These moments of prolixity strike the eye of anyone opening such a book nowadays far more than the marvels and enchantments which we might, even now in the late twentieth century, come to enjoy. But when we do, it may be impossible to feel any special horror reading about the terrible *endriago* (the composite monster which confronts and nearly slays Amadís). The elemental and the demonic have been effectively drained from "primitive" magical tale; magicians, fairies, fantastic animals and castles have, as literature dwindles into a commodity, become mere details of staffage and purveyed technique. The demoniacally evil declines into merely the morally bad, while characters acquire psychological motivations comprehensible to anybody, instead of inscrutable destinies.

A parallel verbosity and sophistication to no purpose accompanies the passage of the pastoral novel through the hands of the purveyors. The invitation, fascinating in the bloodstained sixteenth century, to a world apart where all would be conversation about love and the nobility of souls, became vulgarized in its turn into a pretext for endless and pointless *discreteo*. By this time, as we have remarked earlier, the readers of Spain had made the acquaintance of Heliodorus's great romance, the work which gave definite direction to the purveyors—and also, since there are so many striking things in the Greek novel, to the authors of masterpieces. It was no doubt Gonzalo de Céspedes y Meneses who adapted Heliodorus effectively for the undemanding public, in long sub-litarary fictions full of appeals to the fulfillment of uncomplicated desires and an out-of-place pietism. To Castillo Solórzano, who had read Céspedes, fell the lot of catching this perennial material and the unquenchable effusions of *discreteo* in yet another receptacle: the short novella. For this seems to have been the historical moment, not of a "decline" from the ethos and the subtlety of Cervantes's *Exemplary Novels*, but of the abridgement into companionable format of an ancient purveyed corpus of story.

And from the age of the translation of Castillo into French, Dutch, Italian and English onwards, some aspect of that corpus has always been accessible at the sub-literary level to those who have sought commodity values in the books they buy. The canalizing of social tensions into persiflage at the expense of old-fashioned country gentry may have been one of the most significant movements made in literature towards the invention of the humorist (Sir Roger de Coverley, Uncle Toby, and others in their century); and the power of love, not to endanger the psychic balance of the individual, but to give him or her eventually a place within the organism of society may have led, at a few removes, to the innovations of Richardson. What is even more evident is that this type of fiction predominated without hindrance in an age of political and religious authoritarianism. But in every age and under every form of government, tyrannical or tolerant, purveyed fiction always has.

IV *The Significance of Castillo for Subsequent European Literature*

The continuing significance for readers on Spanish territory of Castillo's work, or indeed the work of any Spanish author of his period with the possible exceptions of Francisco de Quevedo and Baltasar Gracián, is very hard to estimate. One can only surmise that there will be a connection between the rate of the reprintings of any individual author's pieces, either alone, reattributed or in anthologies, and a certain popularity. In Castillo's case these resuscitations of his work were not numerous. Two of his novellas: "The Confusions of a Night" ("La confusión de una noche," from *Los alivios de Casandra*, 1640) and "The Deserved Good Fortune" ("La dicha merecida," from *Sala de recreación*, 1640) were adapted into dramatic form by Agustín Moreto as respectively, *The Confusion of a Garden (La confusión de un jardín)* and *The Deserved Good Fortune (La fortuna merecida)*, but that is about the widest extent of any direct textual influence exerted by Castillo.

The fortunes of his work in literature beyond the frontiers of Spain are much more deserving of examination. Both his comedies and his novellas were able to provoke a veritable *nouvelle vague* all on their own in French narrative fiction. Charles Sorel, in his *Bibliothèque Françoise* (1664), explains the dissatisfaction of the French fiction-reading public with the long, allegorized and universally idealizing romances of the reign of Louis XIII: ". . . *mais les Espagnols nous en donnerent de plus naturelles, et de plus circonstanciées, remplies de naïvetez et d'agrémens*" (". . . but the Spaniards gave us more natural [novellas], better related to circumstances, filled with human touches and moments of amenity").[18] Even a small detail had its importance for the new public, for example the fact that Spanish *novelistas* had shown how a story might be situated at home in Spain, and be given characters with Spanish names instead of those which connoted some impossible Hellenic ideal.[19] So it is that we find borrowings from Castillo in the works of two generations of French authors. Thomas Corneille adapted *The Marquis from the Toledo Suburbs* into *Dom Bertrand de Cigarral*, and Paul Scarron not only transposed *The Lordly Buffoon* into *Dom Japhet d'Arménie* and *L'Héritier Ridicule* but rendered some of Castillo's prose works into inset stories in his *Roman Comique*.[20] The episodes containing the character Destin in the frame-story come from "El ayo de su hijo," and interpolated we find versions of "Los efectos que hace amor," "La confusión de una noche," and "A lo que obliga el honor" and "A un engaño otro mayor" combined into one plot. Direct borrowings by less celebrated authors are usually confined to the theater: Chappuzeau, in this way, turns the Marquina episode of *The She-Stoat of Seville* into *L'Avare Duppé, ou l'Homme de paille* and Montfleury mines his *L'École des Jaloux* out of "El celoso hasta la muerte."[21] Finally Alain-René Le Sage, continuing Scarron's practice of developing the frame-story narrator of a novella as a character, if the figures contained in that story prove incapable of development, appears to derive Dom Alphonse's story in *Gil Blas de Santillane*, IV, 10 from "Más vale el amor que la sangre" and Raphaël's trick in VI, 2 from Domingo's in "El Proteo de Madrid."

France had, it must be pointed out, her own vigorous tradition of novellas beginning with the works of Marguerite de Navarre in the late sixteenth century, and this tradition was by no means eclipsed by the translation and adaptation of the works of Castillo and his contemporaries. The quality of *galanterie* which we find in them is far less reticent, while the circumstances of love and even adultery in these works are distinctly more impudent. At the same time there is a perceptible opening towards the courtly fictional chronicle—scandalous or idealistic—but certainly narrated from a viewpoint impossible for the *académico* Castillo to assume. So it is that the great narratives of Madame de Lafayette, *La Princesse de Montpensier* and *La Princesse de Clèves,* though they bear some historical signs of the reform of the novella under Spanish influence, really reassert a native fictional vigor and escape from the category of novella altogether. The collectons by Préchac, Le Noble and Lesconvel, containing no immediate adaptations from Spanish, continued the tradition in which Castillo had written. By the end of the seventeenth century this, however, was a dying one. The same legacy from Castillo was received in disseminated fashion by Molière and Regnard in the French theater; many relationships between Castillo's buffoons, *cultos* and incompetent doctors and those of Molière cannot be coincidental.

In England the translated works of Castillo imposed themselves on a different society, where above all the novels of swindling were appreciated.[23] These novels, with their lack of expression of disillusion and of real remorse—in contrast with the true *novela picaresca*—spoke to an age of readers of narratives of highwaymen and of scandalous court chronicles. Castillo's works were accepted at the level of purveyed literature along with these.[24] When the English novel eventually arose out of this particular slough in Richardson's *Pamela,* nothing is owed to Castillo's work. Even the choice of a female swindler as chief character of Defoe's *Moll Flanders* may be only a remote tribute to our author.[25] The special mark of Castillo on his longer novels: reprobation of the characters' activities together with sympathy for their irrepressible shamelessness and criminal triumphs, is eloquent of a moral world entirely different from that observed and proposed for remedy by Daniel Defoe.

CHAPTER 7

Castillo as a Poet

ALTHOUGH Castillo's verse has contributed least to his later reputation, it should not be forgotten that it was in the art of satirical poetry that he started out on his literary career. In the cultural world of Castillo's day, moreover, poetry enjoyed a traditional prestige to which works of fiction, lacking Classical antecedents, could not aspire. We may assume, on a more mundane level, that Castillo's situation as an official of a literary academy would also oblige him to produce continuous light entertainment in versified form, if not to aspire to the laurels of the greatest of Spanish poets. Certainly in his verse the reader finds himself on familiar ground; many of the constants in Castillo's thinking permeate it as they do his dramatic and prose works. There is even a more perceptible flavor of life as it was lived in the Madrid of that time, and among the humblest classes; in embryonic form, one might say, we have some *cuadros de costumbres* (sketches of manners) of a type which nineteenth century authors would develop.

In the following pages there is an anthology of Castillo's verse, from *Parnassus Jesting* if it is not otherwise stated. The extraordinary rarity of that book, we feel, justifies this presentation, together with an attempted prose translation into English. Some unusual spellings, which may be of interest to the philologist, are left intact in the Spanish.

Poems of Castillo Solórzano, selected from *Parnassus Jesting* (*Donaires del Parnaso*, 1624) and *Second Part of Tirso de Molina's Comedies* (1635).

I. EN DESPEDIDA DE UNA ACADEMIA QUE SE HACIA EN UNA PIEZA MUY

ON TAKING LEAVE OF A LITERARY ASSEMBLY WHICH MET IN A VERY

79

ESTRECHA, Y LA JORNADA
ERA A CUENCA.

"Academia singular,
docta mansión de las Musas,
de donde ingenios virotes
salen a volar con plumas;
grave oficina de Apolo,
en quien con rigor censuran
todo vicio, todo error
que a sus preceptos repugna;
quinta amena del Parnaso,
que Febo tiene por suya,
aunque por lo que congoja
más parece quinta angustia;
estrechísimo distrito
de la poética turba,
bueno para dar sudores
por lo que tiene de estufa;
hoy un cliéntulo vuestro,
por la gracia de una mula,
se parte a aquella ciudad
que baña el Huécar y el Júcar,
a aquella piña de casas
que en una sierra se funda,
a quien graves edificios
la dura cerviz conculcan.
Pesaroso de dejar
esta Corte, cifra y suma
de lo mejor que contiene
cuanto el rojo Febo alumbra—
aqueste abreviado mapa,
aqueste mar donde sulcan
así los ricos bajeles
como los pobres chalupas—
pena llevo en no gozar
en la academia futura
del aceite con que Apolo
a tantos candiles unta.
Partiendo a ver otros tantos,
por la tierra que chamusca
el sol y cubren celebros
las manchegas caperuzas,
por esos caminos voy

NARROW ROOM. A JOURNEY
TO CUENCA WAS PLANNED

"Peerless academy, learned
dwelling of the Muses, from
whence sally dartlike wits,
borne on their quills; serious
workshop of Apollo in which are
rigorously censured all artistic
vices, all errors which offend
the rules; pleasant country-seat
of Parnassus, which Phoebus
knows as his own—though in
point of asphyxiation it may seem
more like a galley between decks(?);
narrow region of the poetical
throng, perfect for applying the
sweat cure from its resemblance
to a bathhouse; today a minor
client of yours, by the grace
and favor of his mule, leaves you
for that city which Huécar and
Júcar wash with their waters, that
clump of houses set on a hilltop,
the stony neck of which is
weighted down by massive build-
ings.

I am saddened at leaving this
capital city—the compendium and
abridgement of the best contained
in the world which blond Phoebus
shines upon, this *mappamundi* in
little, this sea where both rich
vessels and impoverished sloops
alike
are under weigh—saddened at not
being able to enjoy, in future
academy sessions, the midnight oil
with which Apollo keeps lit so
many lamps.
Leaving as I am to see others,
and crossing the sun-scorched land
where brainpans are covered with

que ya pródigos abundan
si no de fuentes risueñas,
de chanzonetas y pullas—
porque ocupando las hazas
ya la segadora chusma,
tantas espigas derriba
cuantas malicias pronuncia.
Voy por la tierra más calva
que en la Europa se calcula,
sin árbol o planta en ella
que le sirva de verruga.
Por todos los horizontes
ningún arroyo los cruza,
que no hay susurros de arroyos
donde cigarras susurran.
Aquí es Febo cocinero,
pues que de la gente adusta
fríe con sus rayos sesos,
y no fríe que los turra.
No hay defensivo de nieve
a su ardiente calentura,
que la invención de Charquías
nunca esta tierra la usa.
Perdone el señor Apolo
si huyere su faz rotunda,
que a la noche me acomodo
entre buhos y lechuzas.
Pienso ejercitar espuelas
y menudear andaduras,
gozando hasta ver el alba
blanca plata de la luna.
No pretendo que me traiga
la canícula importuna
la subúcula de réquiem,
cuando yo busco alcluyas.
Sea sumiller de corps
con la mauritana turba,
que si para Dios se duerme
para Mahoma madruga.
Así llegaré al lugar
que dos ríos le circundan,
y una casa de moneda
armas de Filipo acuña,
gozando de mal asiento

Manchegan hoods, I set forth over
those roads where there is a
prodigal wealth, if not of smiling
streams, of ribald songs and jibes.
Because now that the swarms of
reapers cover the fields one hears
them utter as many impudences as
ears of wheat they cut down.
I am off across the baldest region
charted in the whole of Europe,
without a tree or a plant by way
of a wart.

From any horizon not a single
brook crosses this land; no brook
murmurs where cicadas are crying.
Here Phoebus is *chef-de-cuisine*,
frying the brains of a swarthy
people, indeed toasting them.
There is no snow to mitigate the
burning heat, as the invention of
Charquías[1] was never put to use
in this place.
May the Lord Apollo forgive me if
I should hide me from the sight
of his rotund face, but at night I
shall take my ease among the owls.

I propose to make use of my spurs
and get the riding done while I
enjoy the pale silver of moonlight,
until the dawn breaks.
I do not wish to provoke the
irksome Dog Star into fitting me
for the garment of lying in state;
I am looking for jubilation.
Let him act as gentleman-of-the-
bedchamber for the Morisco
throng, for they are the ones who,
if they go to sleep for God, wake
up for Muhammad. And so I shall
arrive at that place which two
rivers surround, and where a mint

los edificios que ocupa
como enfermo de almorranas
que no halla parte segura.
Y acabando mi negocio—
poca flema y priesa mucha—
recto trámite me vuelvo
sin buscar más aventuras,
topando mozas gallegas,
ya flacas y ya tetudas,
unas buenas para tabas
y otras buenas para enjundias;
mesoneros socarrones,
que si no desuellan, hurtan;
camas con chinches de arroba
y de a cuarterón las pulgas,
hasta llegar a mi centro
que en pedernales se funda,
y entre su fuego se siembran
los rábanos y lechugas.
Adiós, insignes sujetos,
que un octavario me oculta
desta primera academia
hasta verme en la segunda.
Rogad al cielo que vuelva
con la vena menos zurda,
para ofreceros sainetes
y entreteneros con burlas.
Dijo, y llegando a llamarle
su precursor Pedro Lucas,
subió en la mula y picola,
porque estampase herraduras.

stamps out coins with Philip's
shield on them. Cuenca puts up
with its bad situation like a sufferer
from hemorrhoids, someone who
cannot find a single comfortable
place to settle in.
Once my business is over there,
with little delay and great haste I
shall return directly, looking for
no more adventures, finding by
the wayside Galician lasses, some
thin and some full-breasted, that
is, some good for playing skittles,
others only for rendering down; sly
innkeepers who, if they don't
fleece you, just steal; beds with
bugs by the peck and fleas by the
quarter-pound, until I get back to
Madrid, my true center, founded
on rock, among the fires of which
they plant radishes and lettuces.

Farewell, eminent company, for
eight days I must be parted from
this firstrate academy; a second
week will see me back again. Pray to
heaven that I may return with a
less uncouth wit, to offer you japes
and entertain you
with quips."

So he spoke, and when his
outrider Pedro Lucas appeared
to call him away, he mounted his
mule and spurred her so that
she would leave hoofprints behind.

II. DESCRIBIENDO EN
MADRID UN DÍA DE
ENCIERRO DE TOROS, QUE
FUE EN EL QUE NO LOS

DESCRIBING A DAY OF BULL-
RUNNING IN MADRID, THE
OUTCOME OF WHICH WAS
THAT IT DID NOT TAKE

HUBO, Y LA GENTE SE QUEDÓ BURLADA.

Anticipados holgones,
que atentamente advertís
—como lo hace el calendario—
de las fiestas de Madrid,
hoy la Fama os ha burlado,
que dejando su clarín
por dar voz a la corneta
puso el rostro carmesí.
Si fiastes los que ocupan
un espíritu festín
en su certeza, fue engaño,
que es mujer; sabe mentir.
Al concurso de la fiesta,
ciento a ciento y mil a mil,
gentes de varios estados
pudo el cuidado mullir.
Desvelada la doncella
se encierra en su camarín,
taller de transformaciones,
para transformarse allí.
Con cinco pinceles vivos
y un delgado caniquí
hace hipócrita en colores
al cotidiano país.
Rizo propio o rizo ajeno
—que moño llaman aquí—
saca lleno de más flores
que el almacén de Abril.
Dejar quiso el oficial
el ejercicio servil
que solo le califica
el glorioso San Crispín.
Olvidan dedal y aguja
el sastre y el aprendiz,
desnudos en las conciencias
aunque tratan en vestir.
La damaza que su estado
deriva del vellocín
a caza de forasteros
sale a estafar y a pedir.

PLACE, AND ALL WERE DISAPPOINTED

Intending holidaymakers, you who
take notice, just as the calendar
does, of Madrid's festivals, you
have been cheated today by
Publicity when she put aside her
clarion, played notes on the cornet,
and ended up with a red face. If
you, who have the holiday spirit,
had confidence in her truthfulness,
it was all a delusion: she is female
and knows all about telling fibs.
People from various walks of life
came together in expectation, in a
holiday throng by hundreds and by
thousands. The young girl is
diligent, shutting herself up in her
boudoir, that studio of conversions,
to convert her very self. With five
living brushes and a thin piece of
muslin she makes the everyday
landscape seem as it is not, with
false colorings. She decorates her
own curls, or perhaps those adopted
ones called topknots here, with
more flowers than the storeroom of
April holds. The shoemaker sought
to leave behind him his useful trade,
to which St. Crispin alone lent
dignity. The tailor and his
apprentice leave the thimble and
the needle, their consciences left
without a stitch even though their
trade is in clothing. The fine lady
whose dignity derives from the
"golden fleece" goes out hunting for
visitors to Madrid, to cheat and to
wheedle. The scrivener puts to rest
the goosequill pen which has left so
many hungry, so as to maintain its
own appetite in plenty. The old

Suspende ya el pendolario
el ansarino buril
que a tantos dejó en ayunas
por tener él qué muquir.
Alborózase la anciana,
que es de fiestas zahorí,
y da en fe del negro embozo
vacaciones al monjil.
Sale el lindo con ojeras
del madrugón infeliz,
poseyendo confianzas
y pocos maravedís.
Desvelado el rastrero
en almohazar su rocín,
que al lado de algún señor
ligero ha de competir.
Asegura a doña Urraca
una suerte don Dionís,
imitador de Narciso
enamorado de sí.
Vibra el fresno el mercadante
con vestido de tabí,
transformado en caballero
el que es a pie villejín.
El circo ilustre, que aplaude
cualquier cornígera lid—
que hacer maravilla octava
pretendió todo albañir—
de diferentes estados
de gentes se vio cubrir,
que en circo tal variedad
fue ser cazuela mojí,
cuando por la posta llegan,
sin prevención de cojín,
la Fama y el Desengaño
dando a todos qué sentir.
Desvaneciose la fiesta:
toda empanada y pernil
que no sirvió para toros
vino en merienda a servir.
Tal hubo que el mediodía
le cogió hecho matachín
más colmado de esperanzas
que en su ley está un rabí,[2]

woman, that diviner of festivals, is
restless, and gives a vacation to the
widow's garb, now concealed
beneath her black shawl. The
man-about-town sets out, his eyes
encircled after an ill-timed
hangover, prodigal of promises, but
having little ready cash. The meat
carter is diligent too, throwing a
blanket over his jade, for later he
will have to compete shamelessly at
the side of some notable. Don
Dionís assures Doña Urraca of the
chances of a wager, though he
imitates Narcissus in being really in
love with himself. The merchant in
his suit of tabby brandishes an
ash-hafted pike transformed into a
knight on his mount, while on foot
he is no more than a clodhopper (?).
The seated circle of notables, which
will applaud any contest involving
horned beasts —for every
stonemason pretended he was to
perform the eighth wonder of the
world—now consisted of all ranks of
people; such variety on the benches
turned them into a veritable
salmagundi. Then, posthaste, arrive
Rumor and Disappointment,
causing sorrow to all. The festival
melted away; all the pies and ham
which were to have been served at
the bullfight went to provide
ordinary luncheons. Some there
were who were caught perplexed at
midday, like men on the high-wire,
more burdened with the waiting
than a rabbi is in his religion, until
Lord Apollo, that harlequin tumbler
along his ecliptic, forced them to
leave the square like all the others.
The disappointed ones, in
quarrelsome tumult, made a vow

hasta que el señor Apolo,
de su eclíptico Arlequín,
a él como a los demás
de la plaza hizo salir.
Prometieron los burlados,
en rebelado motín,
de no salir más a encierros
sin su certeza advertir.

not to turn up again for bullfights
unless they might be sure they
would actually happen.

III. AL DESDEN FINGIDO DE UN AMANTE, POR DISIMULAR SU FAVOR

ON THE FEIGNED INDIFFERENCE OF A LOVER, CONCEALING HIS AFFECTION

Como el fingido hipócrita sagaz,
que con pálidos visos en la tez,
y con el saco estrecho, hace juez
al mundo que es un santo montaraz;
como, en su vanagloria pertinaz,
desea acreditarse que tal vez
    come solas dos pasas y una nuez,
cuando aventaja al bruto más voraz;
    asi un galán, de amor más que
        aprendiz,
gozando de su mesa el dulce arroz,
poner quiere a sus gustos un telliz.
    Halago miente, publicando coz;
desdenes zapes sin consuelo miz,
siendo en tacto Esaú, Jacob en voz.

Just as the feigning, crafty
hypocrite, who, with a face all pallid
and a narrow, tight doublet, leaves
the world of the opinion that he is a
saint of the wilderness; and just as in
his obstinate vanity, he wishes to
have it said of him that on occasion
he dines on merely two raisins and a
walnut, when really he could put to
shame the most voracious of
animals; so a certain lover, more
than a mere apprentice in love's art,
and enjoying the sweet morsels of
love's table, seeks to slide a
saddlecloth under his delight for it
to ride on. He dissembles
attentiveness by making an outward
show of rudeness, of snappish
disdain with no consoling cossets;
let us say he is rough Esau to the
touch and smooth Jacob in his voice.

IV. ENIGMA

AN ENIGMA

¿Cuál es el muerto animal
que entre vivos se conserva,

What is: an inanimate beast which
flourishes among the living, and

y a sus dueños les reserva
del rigor del temporal?
Arrástranle, y no hace mal;
es llevado con rigor;
es persona de rumor;
viste caro y cuesta mucho;
no es ave, fiera, aguilucho,
perro, mono ni atambor.
En cualquier calle se mete,
aunque por virtud ajena;
es cosa que no da pena;
sirve de una vez a siete;
es un callado alcahuete,
de mujeres estimado;
no pace, aunque cursa el Prado
en verano y por enero;
trae cortinas; no es barbero;
cursos hace, y no es purgado.
Plinio nunca investigó
déste tal la propiedad,
que sola mi habilidad
por COCHE le conoció.
Por aquéste se olvidó
cursar una y otra silla.
Ya el caballo no se ensilla,
que es comodidad más sana
una salchicha alazana,
y una morcilla morcilla.

keeps his owners from the force of
the wind; is dragged along, but
doing no harm; is conveyed
pitilessly; has a personality which
gets noised abroad; is well dressed
and costly; is neither bird, wild
animal, eaglet, dog, monkey nor
drum.
Pushes himself into any street, even
though by others' efforts; is a thing
which stirs no compassion; can be
used by seven at a time; is a most
silent pander appreciated by
women; is never put out to grass,
even though striding through the
Prado in summer or in January;
carries curtains, but isn't a barber;
makes runs, but not from any effect
of a purge? Pliny never studied the
characteristics of this animal; my
cleverness alone knew it to be a
COACH.
Following "courses" with either
"chair" in mind is now forgotten
because of this animal. Nobody now
saddles a horse for riding; a
horse-drawn sausage, or a roan
bloodpudding is more convenient
and safe.

V. A LA FUERZA DE LUCRECIA, REFERIDA POR JULIA, DUEÑA DE SU CASA, GLOSANDO PRINCIPIOS DE ROMANCES.[3]

ON THE RAPE OF LUCRETIA, TOLD BY JULIA HER *DUENNA*, GLOSSING THE OPENING LINES OF OLD BALLADS

De Lucrecia contaré
la historia, pues fui testigo,
y a todo siempre me hallé
yo que lo sé, que lo vi se lo digo;

I shall tell the story of Lucretia,
since I was a witness and was
present at all times. I who know
shall tell you what I saw; I who tell

yo que lo digo lo vi, que lo sé.
Junto a Roma, no en Turquía,
que es muy diferente ley
y distinta monarquía,
de caza se vino el Rey
bien así como solía.
Diole Lucrecia a cenar,
hízole cama de flores,
mas desnudo en tal lugar
Conde Claros[4] *con amores*
no podía reposar.
Hecho el vientre un atambor,
daba vueltas por el lecho
diciendo el rey comedor:
—Esto que me abrasa el pecho
no es posible que es amor.
Amor le dijo:—Mentís,
que estáis de amor abrasado.
Y él replicó, si advertís:
—Las tres de la noche han dado,
corazón, y no dormís.
Parte a recibir mercedes
de quien puede a manos llenas,
y entró a dilatar sus redes
en un retrete que apenas
se divisan las paredes.
Pasos siente del galán
en su aposento la dama,
y por si asalto la dan
salto diera de la cama
que parece un gavilán.
El la dijo:—Hermoso alcaide
deste vuestro corazón,
bella Zaida deste Zaide,
solos a que en confesión
que nos escucha nadie.
Este tierno Durandarte,
si no te causan enojo,
de sus penas te da parte.
¡Agua va! ¡Que las arrojo!
¡Todo cristiano se aparte!
Si escuchar quieres mis penas
ya descubro la tramoya,
pues por tus luces serenas

you saw it, for I know it.
Near to Rome—not in Turkey,
which has a quite different religion
and monarchy—King Tarquin came
back from the hunt, just as he
always did.
Lucretia gave him his supper and
made him a flower strewn bed. But,
naked in that spot, "Conde Claros"
could not find rest because of love.
With his inward parts drumming,
the well-fed king tossed on the bed,
and said: "It is impossible that this
thing which sears my breast should
be love."
But Love told him: "You are wrong;
you are indeed burned by love."
Tarquin replied (and note this well):
"It is already three o'clock, my
heart, and still you will not sleep."
So he gets up to receive his bliss
from that one who can bestow it
bountifully, going in to spread his
snares in a chamber where it is
hardly possible to make out the
walls. The lady hears the lover's
steps in her room and, foreseeing
that she might be attacked, leapt
like a hawk from the bed.
Said Tarquin: "Beautiful castellan of
this your heart, fair Zaida of this
Zaide, now that we are alone and
can confess, no one can hear us.
This gentle Durandarte tells you of
his pain, if such a thing does not
cause you irritation.
Water below! I'm hurling down my
grief! Let everyone stand clear!
If you will listen to my plaints I shall
reveal the whole scheme to you. For
Troy is burning, its towers, edifices
and ramparts set afire by your
serene eyes."
She replies: "You come very

ardiendo se estaba Troya,
torres, cimientos y almenas.
—Necio venís para alcalde,
le responde, ¿Cuándo en cueros
dije: 'Este cuerpo tomalde'
a los moros por dineros,
y a los cristianos de balde?
Las entraños lastimadas
dejó al rey, y con temor
dijo a sus luces airadas:
—¡Ay verdades, que en amor
siempre fuistes desdichadas!
Duélate la pena mía,
que al fin no es pena plebeya,
que diré viéndote impía:
—'Mira Nero de Tarpeya
a Roma cómo se ardia'.
Dame gustos, no pesares,
que si no, vendrán de Fez
a que me admitas y ampares
ocho a ocho y diez a diez
Sarracinos y Aliatares.
Con el verse amenazar
sus fuerzas se le rindieron,
que vienen a aventajar
lágrimas que no pudieron
tanta dureza ablandar.
Cesaron sus travesuras,
según afirman poetas,
que a esparcir nieblas oscuras
el mayor de los planetas
convidaba a las criaturas.
Viendo al sol abrir postigo
en el balcón turquesado,
en camisa y sin abrigo,
de las batallas cansado
se sale el Rey Rodrigo.
Vistiose a priesa, aunque lacio,
por partirse, que malsines
le dijeron que su espacio
murmuraban los rocines
a las puertas de palacio.
La que ya no se resiste,
sintiendo su ligereza,

unwisely, for a governor of men, for
when did I ever say: 'Take this
naked body' either to Moors (for
payment) or to Christians (gratis)?"
This left the king with an inward
anguish, and fearfully he declared,
before her angry gaze: "Alas,
sincerity in matters of love, ever did
you bring misfortune." May my
sufferings strike pity in you, for
truly it is no plebeian sorrow. I must
say, seeing how unkind you are:
"Nero looks down from the Tarpeian
Rock at how Rome burns. Give me
contentment, not grief; if not, from
Fez will come Saracens and
Aliatares by eights and tens to make
you look on me with favor."
Seeing herself threatened, her
resistance came to an end, and tears
which had been unable to overcome
such cruelty now show to her
beauty's advantage.
The revels of this pair came to their
end, as authoritative poets tell us,
when the greatest of the planets
invited all created things to scatter
darkness away.
Observing the sun opening a
skylight in his turquoise balcony,
"King Rodrigo," exhausted from his
encounter and unclad but for his
shirt, emerges.
He quickly puts on his clothes,
albeit loosely, to make good his
escape, for evil tongues told him
that his very horses were
complaining at the palace gates of
his tardiness.
She who now no longer resisted,
regretting past wantonness, says
while she dresses herself: "No other
sad wight's sorrow can compare with
mine."

dice al tiempo que no se viste:
—*Competir con mi tristeza*
no puede la de otro triste.
　Afligida la dejaron
los recuerdos de la boda,
mas sus ojos lo pagaron,
que en peso la noche toda
sin cesar clamorearon.
—Tan aleves falsedades,
dice, lloren mis zafiros,
sintiendo mis liviandades,
aquí donde mis suspiros
pueblan estas soledades.
　Y aborreciéndos así,
con una daga acerada
se dio muerte, aunque acudí,
la bella malmaridada,
de las más lindas que vi.
　Así murió esta matrona,
mordaz que muerdes y aun comes,
porque no excepta persona
la que a ninguno perdona,
al rey ni a sus ricos homes.

Memories of that union left her
grieving, but her eyes atoned for
this, for all night they wept without
ceasing.
She said: "May my sapphire eyes
weep for such traitorous behavior,
and for my lustfulness, here where
my sighs alone fill these lonely
places."
And hating herself in this way the
beautiful ill-married lady, one of the
prettiest I have seen, slew herself
with a steel poniard, although I
myself ran to help.
So died this Roman matron. Bitter
death, you who sting and even
devour! For death makes no
exceptions, sparing nobody, neither
kings nor great nobles of the land.

VI. [QUEJAS DEL MANZANARES]

El espejo de cristal
que al Alcázar de Filipo
le sirve entero el invierno
y quebrado en el estío,
el que por no ser arroyo
es ya sincopado río,
en cuyas aguas de jaspe
se cometen ranicidios,
querelloso, y con razón,
que le olviden cuando rico
y le busquen cuando pobre,
aquesto a la Corte dijo:
—Señora doña Madrid,
sepa que estoy ofendido
que para mí sea madrastra
la madre de tantos hijos.

THE COMPLAINT OF THE MANZANARES

That glassy mirror which reflects
Philip's citadel, in one piece in the
winter and in fragments in the
summer, and which, so as not to
dwindle into being a mere brook,
turns itself into a river by fits and
starts—in the opaque jasper waters
of which massacres of frogs take
place—in an offended tone, and
rightly so, for people do forget him
when he is wealthy and seek him
out when he has least, addressed
Madrid thus: "Lady Madrid, let it
be known that I am offended that
the mother of so many citizens
should be a stepmother to me. What

¿Qué me quiere en mi pobreza,
pues con el calor estivo
el barrio de Lavapiés
le traslada a mi distrito?
Gentes de varios estados
alivian calor conmigo,
sin tener apenas uno
con quien yo tuviera alivio.
Solaz dicen que les dan
mis fragmentos cristalinos,
cuando parezco destrozo
de algún camarín de vidrios.
Correspondo a la intención
del que a buscarme ha venido,
pues si ríe de mis faltas
yo de las suyas me río.
El jarifo que pretende
verse en mis aguas jarifo
tan a pedazos se mira
que no imitara a Narciso.
La damaza, que al afeite
toda su fama ha debido,
piensa ser ninfa en mis aguas,
y bañada, es cocodrilo.
Dama he visto en mi ribera
de metales más distintos
que la estatua que erigió
aquel rey de los asirios.[5]
¡Cuántas deben a sus faldas
el tener tantos rendidos,
que depuestas les notaran
los defetos que averiguo!
¡Cuántas crespas de copete,
secuaces del artificio,
por no lo estar en mis aguas
dejan en casa los rizos!
¡Cuántas cojas, cuántas zambas
en mi término registro,
que le deben más al corcho
que no al padre que les hizo!
Del pasado lavatorio
a la mañana me miro
cual tablilla de pintor
o como alquicel morisco.

does she want of me in my poverty,
that she should transfer the whole
district of Lavapiés to my purlieus
because of the summer heat? People
of the several social orders allay
their heat with me, when I possess
hardly one fathom in which to allay
my own. They say that my crystal
fragments give them solace, just
when I look like the debris of a
showcase of glassware. I meet the
requirements of everyone who
seeks me out; there are those who
laugh at my defects, and I laugh at
theirs.

The man of fashion who fancies he
sees himself reflected in all his
modishness in my waters, finds
himself so separated into pieces that
he is unable to imitate Narcissus.
The fine lady who owes all her fame
to cosmetics thinks she will play the
nymph in my stream, but once she
has taken her bath she is more like a
crocodile. I've seen a wench on my
banks of more diverse metals than
the statue set up by that Assyrian
king. How many of these owe to the
generosity of their skirts the fact
that they captivate so many of those
who might observe, once their
ladies were unskirted, those defects
which I am well aware of! How
many madams of the courtly
coiffures, followers of artifice, leave
those curls at home so as not to
become hydraulic water movers!
How many lame ones, bowlegged
ones I glimpse in my domain, who
are more indebted to cork soles than
to the fathers who begot them! After
this morning ablution has taken
place I am left bespattered like a

En mí hacen sus conciertos,
sus ventas y sus esquilmos,
donde es su capa la noche
como a maula en baratillo.
Como callados nos hallan
a mí, al Soto y los molinos,
al paso que el calor crece
acrecientan sus delitos.
Confesores de Madrid,
apercibid los oídos,
que os espera gran cosecha
si os dicen lo que hemos visto."

painter's palette or a Morisco's cape.
On my banks people make their
agreements, their sales and their
harvests, where night is their cloak,
like the lookout at a thieves' market.
Since they find we all hold our
tongues, myself, the Soto and the
watermills, their mischief increases
in volume with the heat. Confessors
of Madrid, prick up your ears. A
great access of riches awaits you if
you ever get to hear of what we have
seen."

VII. A LOS MIRONES DE UNA ACADEMIA.

TO THE LOOKERS-ON AT A LITERARY GATHERING

Exploradores eternos,
que en el garito de Apolo,
por faltaros el caudal,
miráis mucho y jugáis poco;
los que en el juego de cientos
"de la baraja" os apodo:
a los treses, que no sirven;
a los nueves y a los ochos;
venir a sólo mirar
es lo que me causa asombro,
pecando vuestros ingenios
nada en linces, mucho en topos.
Si viniérades al tiempo
que el sol dora el Capricornio,
y por topar con Acuario
lleva el carro presuroso,
sirviérades en la sala—
aunque es su distrito corto—
de figuras de tapices:
mucho abrigo y poco estorbo.
Mas cuando el ardiente Can,
anhelante y congojoso,
centellas vomita ardientes
para chamuscar rastrojos,
es dar al calor de Febo,

Everlasting explorers, who in
Apollo's gaming den look on a great
deal yet, through lack of resources,
play little; you who in the game of
"hundreds" I would describe as
undealt cards: useless threes, nines
and eights;
it astonishes me that you come only
to look on, for your wits remind me
less of the sharp-eyed lynx than of
the unenlightened mole. If you
were to arrive at that season of the
year when the sun is in Capricorn
and hastening along his chariot
towards Aquarius I might compare
you to figures in a tapestry, draped
about the walls of the room—small
though it is—keeping things warm
and not obtruding. But when the
blazing Dog Star, panting and out of
breath, puffs out flaming sparks and
singes the harvests, it is as though
you are unleashing a heatwave upon
Phoebus's fire itself, all because of
your inert presence, or shall we say

con vuestro enfado, buchorno,
y a las desnudas paredes
una simera de forros.
Solo el que fiscalice
ha menester poner ojos
a la objeción del poema,
sobrando los de vosotros.
¿No es compasión que un barbado
tenga apariencia de docto,
y a título de mirón
pase plaza de curioso?
¡Qué es mirarle la fachada
a un circunspecto honoroso [sic]
mostrando filos de agudo,
y experimentado, es boto!
Aquí se me ofrece un cuento
para los mirones todos—
perdonen si fuere largo;
verán cuan bien le acomodo.
Salió para decir misa
a un altar un religioso,
destos en presteza rayos,
destos en la flema soplos.
Dejó encendidas las velas
el ministro cuidadoso,
el misal en el atril,
y fuese a ayudar a otro.
Sucediole en su lugar,
en buenos paños, un mozo,
con el rosario en la mano,
arrodillado y devoto.
Y en fe de que su cuidado
estaba a ayudarle prompto,
comenzó el fraile la misa
en alto y sonoro tono.
En diciendo el *Introibo*
halló falto el responsorio
del monacillo barbado,
y presumió que era sordo.
Mirole el preste a la cara,
y alzando la voz un poco,
tornó al principio del salmo
y hallose en decirlo solo.
Díjole:—Señor galán,

a frieze of warm hangings on the
walls. Only the member who is
actually criticizing a poem need
follow the examination of it with his
eyes; your glances are superfluous.
Is it not a pitiful thing to see some
bearded fellow with the appearance
of a sage acquire the reputation of
being erudite, when he has only
looked on? What a shame it is to
observe some simulacrum of a
critical eminence showing the
"sharp edge of his wit," when one
finds out later on that it is quite
blunt! Here a story occurs to me,
one applicable to all lookers-on.
(Forgive me if it's a long one; it will
be seen how I make it stick). A
certain friar set out to say mass in a
chapel, one of those friars who are
lightning in punctuality and puffing
with impatience. The deacon had
arranged for candles to be lit and the
missal to be on the lectern, and had
gone off to assist someone else. In
his place there appeared a well
dressed youth, who knelt devoutly
with rosary in hand. So, assuming
that this fellow was his assistant, the
friar began to sing mass in a loud,
sonorous voice. While saying the
Introibo he did not catch the
response the bearded acolyte should
have made, and presumed that the
fellow was deaf. The priest looked
him in the face and, raising his voice
somewhat, went back to the
beginning of the psalm. Again he
found himself alone in saying it.
He said: "Young man, do you not
know how to serve mass?." The
other replied: "Father, don't let this
fine attire deceive you. I do not
really know how to, but I just offer

¿no sabe ayudarme?—El otro
le respondió:—Padre mío,
no le engañe aqueste adorno,
que no sé ayudar a misa.
que en este puesto me pongo
por tocar la campanilla—
porque con gracia la toco."
Aplicado a los mirones
—pidiendo perdón—conozco
que sólo para mirar
se han venido tras nosotros.
Mas si vienen otro día
haré que el dios luminoso,
protector de los tudescos—
con barba y cabellos rojos—
traiga una centuria dellos
(después de brindarse a Morro)
a que despejen la sala,
sin dejar hombre solo.
Cañas hay cada semana;
en el parque corren toros;
vayan a mirar sus suertes;
dense buen cebo a los ojos.
Y si piensa ser poeta
alguno, es intento loco,
que no le admiten las Musas
al cerrado de meollo.
Dejen libre la academia,
que su calor es dañoso,
y el celebro de un poeta
corre peligro notorio.
Esta es la primer [*sic*] censura,
porque monseñor Rodolfo
me ha de dar una paulina
que los excomulgue a todos.

myself for the job so that I may
tinkle the bell. I have such a talent
for tinkling."
When this is applied to our
lookers-on (And here I beg your
forgiveness) I realize they have
followed our fortunes merely to be
nonparticipants. But, if they turn up
another day, I shall see to it that the
sun-god, protector of the
Germans—having the same blond
beard and hair—shall bring here a
hundred of them (once they have
paid their respects to Sir Gullet).
They will clear the hall and leave
not one of them in it. There are
equestrian shows every week, and
bull-running in the park is there to
see. Let them all go to try their luck
and feast their eyes. And if any one
of them has ambitions to be a
poet . . . what a crazy thought! For
the Muses will never admit to their
presence anyone who is weak in the
understanding. Let these
nonparticipants not clutter up our
academy, because the heat they
generate is harmful, and the poet's
brain is notoriously susceptible to
excess heat. This is the first
warning. Monsignor Rodolfo will
supply me with a note of
excommunication meant expressly
for them.

VIII. A UNA DAMA, QUE NO
PIDIENDO, RECEBIA [*SIC*]
CUANTO LE DABAN.

TO A LADY WHO WOULD
ACCEPT EVERYTHING GIVEN
HER, ALTHOUGH NEVER
MAKING REQUESTS

Filis, si con no pedir
el uso quieres torcer,
advierte que viene a ser

Phyllis, if you wish to break with the
custom by not actually asking for
things, please realize that accepting

punto menos recebir.
Mal te puedes excluir
que añades en cada acción
fuerzas a la obligación,
y cuando en cobrar las hago
me permites el amago,
y a otro le ejecución.

things amounts to nearly the same.
You can scarcely exclude yourself
from the rule that obligations
increase in force with every action
you take. Yet when I take some
action towards collecting a
quid-pro-quo, I find that I am
allowed the preliminary gesture,
but someone else is allowed the real
thing.

IX. PINTANDO A UN TORO EN LA PLAZA Y LA RIZA [*SIC*] QUE HACE.

PORTRAYING A BULL IN THE SQUARE AND THE LAUGHTER HE CAUSES.

¡Guarda, guarda, plebeya tabahola!
Mira que sale del toril un rayo,
que con rigor dos puntas enarbola,
amenazando todo fiel lacayo.
Este, para llevar cuatro de bola,
a toda furia corre son desmayo,
tarugos clava y echa melecinas
en las ancas que topa más vecinas.

Look out, look out, plebeian throng!
See how a flash of lightning has set
itself free from its stall, a bull who
angrily brandishes his points, a
threat to every true servingman.
This bull, trying to carry off four at a
time, runs in full fury intent upon
prodding wooden dummies and
injecting medicine into whatever
haunches he can find nearest to
    him.

*

Los agudos puñales de azabache
empleó rigurosos en el buche
de un morillo que vino de Alarache
a ser de sus dos puntas el estuche.
Temiendo cada cual que le
    despache,
no hay quien de cerca su bramido
    escuche;
de oficio de figones se aprovecha,
que toda pierna liberal amecha.

*

Angrily he puts to work his sharp
poniards, black as jet, in the guts of
a little Moor, come all the way from
Al-Araish just to be the case for
these two scalpels to repose in.
Everyone fears he may be next to be
dispatched; no one stays to listen to
the bellowing from close by. They
all "set the fuse" to their legs,
(rather as the catamites may be said
to do).

*

A un lacayo embistió, que su librea
le da mayores filos a sus ganas
a quien más en sus cuernos ver desea
    sotanas.
De un topetón le afea.
puees necesita ya de dos botanas.

*

He attacked one servingman, since
your lackey's livery puts a sharper

Testigos hizo a muchos del suceso.
dándole el sol donde le dio a
don Bueso.[6]

*

Fuego arrojan los ojos, que sañudos
los pone en dos caballos, y ligero
parte a hacer de sus vientres dos
    menudos—
    que es el toro excelente
    mondonguero.
De los rejones en defensa duros
no teme los rigores del acero,
Caballos destripó, dueños derriba
y cada capa la convierte en criba.

*

Desclavose un asiento de un tablado
donde estaba una vieja, y en la plaza
cayó cerca del toro, que indignado
de sus secretas partes hizo plaza:
cogiola y arrojola en un terrado
como si fuera de papel de estraza—
señal de que el torillo fuerzas tiene,
o de que la mentira es muy solene.

edge on his fury; he'd rather spit
this on his horns than four hundred
pairs of cassocks. With one thrust he
ruins the spangled silk, and a pair of
patches becomes needful. The
lackey had many witnesses in this
case; the sun lit up the same part
which Don Bueso exposed in his
time.

*

His eyes dart fire as he wrathfully
directs them at the horses, and off
he goes to reduce their bellies to
tripe—for your bull is an excellent
tripe dresser. He has no fear of the
merciless steel of defensive lances.
He disemboweled horses, throws off
their riders and makes a sieve of
every cloak.

*

A seat on which an old woman was
sitting came loose from the
platform, and she fell down into the
square, right next to the bull. He, in
his indignation, made a
demonstration of her hidden parts,
picking her up and hurling her on to
a rooftop as though she had been
made of wrapping paper. This is an
instance either of a very strong bull
or of the incorrigibility of liars.

X. [QUEJAS DE LA ESPOSA DEL MANZANARES]

La esposa que a Manzanares
en vez de mano dio el pie
esto le dice a su esposo,
cansada de lo que es:
—Menguado consorte mío,

A CURTAIN-LECTURE FOR THE MANZANARES

The woman who gave the
Manzanares not her hand in
marriage, but rather her foot, tired
of his disposition, says this to her
husband: "Worn-out husband of

de quien vine a ser mujer
forzada y hecha pedazos,[7]
sin por qué ni para qué,
infante arroyo nacistes,
y si riachuelo os veis,
es por ser siempre mendigo
como importuno irlandés.
¿Cuándo esperanza de rico
en posesión trocaréis,
que está en vos más dilata
que en el pueblo de Israel?
Menos parias os tributa
el cano Puerto después
que tiraniza sus copos
de Charquías el poder.
Ya de la fuente de Isidro
ningún socorro esperéis,
que la usurpan sus cristales
las tercianas y la sed.
Vuestros olmos en estío
dicen al que os llega a ver
en lugar de 'Aquí fue Troya',
'Aquí Manzanares fue'.
Por lo flaco y trasijado
hidalgo venías a ser,
mas en lo ambicioso de agua
labrador me parecéis.
Aunque el título de río
llegastes a merecer,
ha sido sin posesiones,
pues estado aún no tenéis.
En esto de agasajar
no es general vuestro bien,
pues por admitir las ranas
despedís a todo pez.
Vuestra playa mantuana,
de lavanderas taller,
ya en lo turbio, ya en lo claro,
es glosa de todos pies.[8]
Sus embajadas os hacen
por deudo que contraéis
de Valladolid, Esgueva,
de Medina, Zapardiel.
Cada cual de la inmundicia

mine, of whom I became the wife by
force and after ill-treatment, all
without rhyme or reason, may I
remind you that you were born a
prince among brooks, and if you
now seem to be just a muddy creek
it is because you will not give up
begging like a feckless Irishman.
When do you propose to exchange
those expectations of riches for the
real thing? Because you show more
dilatoriness than the ever-expectant
nation of Israel.
The white-haired mountain pass of
Guadarrama pays you a smaller
tribute now that the activities of
Charquías make their claims on the
snow there. Don't expect any help
from the fountain of San Isidro;
tertian agues and thirsty people
make demands on its waters too. In
high summer the neighboring elms
announce for all to hear not: 'Here
stood Troy', but rather 'Here was
Manzanares'.
Through debility and skinniness you
were indeed once quite the *hidalgo*,
though in your greed to get hold of a
water supply you seem to me more
like a peasant. Although you
eventually came to deserve the title
of river, it was a title bereft of
demesnes; you have nothing to
support it with. For a man who
entertains guests, you aren't lavish
with good things, since you say
farewell to all fishes just to make
room for the frogs. Your Mantuan
shore, workplace of laundresses,
provides a 'gloss' for every 'foot',
thanks to an intermittent clarity.
Embassies visit you, on matters
dynastic, from the river Esgueva at
Valladolid and the Zapardiel at

cherrión undoso es,
mas vos disfrazada en lienzo
la pretendéis expeler.
De mis ojos y narices
compasión pueden tener,
pues huye dellos el llanto,
y el romadizo también.
Salid de pobre, buen río,
pedid que instrución os dé
el que hoy miráis con hacienda
y pobre vistes ayer.

Medina del Campo. Each of them is
a cart carrying away ordure in liquid
form, but you are the only one who
tries to get rid of it in the guise of
laundered linen. They must show
some sympathy for my eyes and
nostrils, since neither tears nor
catarrh will liquefy now. Give up
these poor man's habits, river, and
pray that someone whom you now
see wealthy and who yesterday was
a pauper may give you some
advice."

XI. A LAS NOVEDADES DE MADRID.

NEWFANGLED THINGS IN MADRID

Madrid, de naciones madre,
apercibe los oídos,
porque el licenciado Momo
pide la pluma a Zoilo.[9]
El publicar tus defetos
más es virtud que no vicio,
pues te pone la ceniza
porque moderes lo altivo.
A ti el señor Manzanares,
con presunciones de río,
te ofrece media corona
como de monje benito.
Tal vez te la da de fraile
cuando es prodigio invernizo,
hasta que llega a raparla
el barbero del estío.
Estase madama puente
sin lavarse el oculismo,
con arenosas lagañas
y esperanzas de judío.
Diversos coches pasean
llenos de ninfas y ninfos
tu Calle Mayor, errantes
sin llevar intento fijo.
Coches hay azotacalles—
y aquí entra bien el distingo:
si, por cubiertos de lodo,

Madrid, mother of nations, prick up
your ears, now that the satiric
Momus is taking over the pen of the
critical Zoilus.
Publicizing your defects is rather a
virtuous than a shameful thing,
asking you to wear ashes on your
head so that you'll moderate that
vainglory. To you Sir Manzanares,
presuming that he's quite a river,
offers at least half of a crown (like a
Benedictine's tonsure). Sometimes,
as some prodigious winter bounty,
he'll crown you with the full,
Franciscan, one—until summer
comes as a barber to shear it all off.
Madam Bridge hasn't been able to
wash her eyes of the sandy dirt left
in them; she shows the patience of
the Jews.
Plenty of coaches pass here, laden
with nymphs male and female,
along your Calle Mayor, on the
move without fixed destinations.
There are some street-punishing
coaches, and here it will be as well
to bring out the query: Are they,

son coches o son cochinos.
Coches hay cuyos caballos
macerados en su tiro
con el hipo de cebada
nunca serán hipogrifos.
Están las gradas del santo
que a Cristo imitó en martirio
con plenitud cotidiana
de soldados y zuizos.
Aquí la propia alabanza
se ha hecho común estilo,
no dando libranza en plumas
de Homeros ni Tito Livios.
Naturaleza se queja
agraviada, porque ha visto
que ya las cinturas andan
apóstatas de su sitio:
porque, con el uso nuevo,
quitan el polvo al olvido
del primero que cantó:
Mediodía era por filo.
Pero llegando a las damas,
ya que su San Juan les vino,
su frecuencia contaré
de disfraces inauditos.
¡Qué es ver un cabello padre
cubierto con otro hijo,
si mártir en lo rizado,
confesor en lo postizo!
Con transformarse los rostros,
a poder del artificio,
el primero ser desmienten
y enfrenan el apetito.
Mujer hubo que en su boda
otra la vio su marido
a la siguiente mañana,
conque descasarse quiso.
(Pienso yo sin duda alguna
que aquesto tuvo principio
para negar una deuda,
o escaparse de un castigo).
Hecha devoción la gala,
por profanar lo divino,
son hábitos y retablos

covered with mire as they are,
road-hogs or just hogs? Coaches
there are whose horses, in bad
shape after the pulling they've
done, will never attain to being
hippogriffs with the broken wind.
The church steps of St.
Philip's—that saint who suffered the
same martyrdom as Christ—are
every day crowded with troopers
and footsoldiers.
Here hyperbole is become the
commonest style of speaking, no
longer being set aside for the pen of
a Homer or a Livy. Nature
complains of the outrage done to
her, now that she's seen waistlines
moving heretically out of their
places. Since the new fashions came
in they are dusting off the memory
of that poet who sang: "It was
exactly in the middle of the day. . ."
But, coming now to the matter of
the ladies, now that their
Midsummer has arrived, I shall
describe their enthusiasm for
unusual disguises. What a shameful
thing it is to see old man natural hair
covered up by young man periwig!
Hair is like a martyr by virtue of the
torments applied to it, but like a
confessor . . . of its own
fraudulence. With the
transformation of their faces, the
result of this faking, they give away
their true natures, and become less
appetizing also. Once there was a
woman who seemed to be one thing
on her wedding day and something
quite different the day after, so that
her husband wanted to dissolve the
marriage (I myself believe quite
genuinely that all this disguising had
its origin in somebody wanting to

lo más nuevo y más jarifo.
Imitan a los venteros,
que en su venta el menos pío
tiene, desollando a todos,
lamparilla y crucifijo.
Son vendederas de plaza,
que pagan a un ciego amigo
que les rece por los muertos
mientras que roban los vivos.
En todo son variables;
sólo firmes las he visto
en aquesto del pedir,
sicut erant in principio.

avoid a creditor, or to escape from
the arm of the law). Finery has
become devotion through the
profaning of religious articles. What
is now most fashionable and most
resplendent has become the new
sacred vestment, the new retable to
be adored. The ladies of Madrid are
like innkeepers, the least devout of
whom has in his establishment a
burning lamp and a crucifix, even
when he's skinning all the guests
alive. They are like market-women,
who pay a friendly blind man to say
prayers for their departed ones,
while they themselves "rob blind"
the living. In all things women are
changeable creatures; I've only seen
them resolute in one thing:
wheedling—as they were ever since
Eve.

XII-1. AL SUCESO DE UN
NOVIO QUE TROCO LA NOCHE
DE SU BODA UNA BEBIDA CON
LA PURGA DE UN ENFERMO.

ON THE OCCASION OF A
BRIDEGROOM'S MISTAKING,
ON HIS WEDDING NIGHT, AN
INVALID'S PURGE FOR A
CORDIAL

Para el tálamo nupcial
pretende esfuerzos un novio,
donde créditos de viejo
desmientan obras de mozo.
De una confección se vale,
con quien impulsos briosos
la familia de los Flacos
trocasen por la de Osorios.[10]
Con la purga de un enfermo
menos caballo y más potro,
hizo un trueque el boticario,
desdescuidado o malicioso.
La prevención del tomarla
no fue con acuerdos de otro,
que en advertencias ajenas
no libra cuidados propios.

A certain bridegroom had hopes of
great results in the nuptial bed,
where the realities of senility might
be contradicted by a "youthful"
performance. He has recourse to a
concoction by virtue of which fiery
impulses might cause the clan of the
Flacci to be mistaken for the daring
Osorios. The apothecary, either in
error or as a prank, exchanged this
aphrodisiac for the purge of an
invalid, less cocksure and more in
torment. The precaution of taking
this draught had been divulged to
nobody by the bridegroom, for he
doesn't wish to bring his

La novia, con esperanzas
de restaurar el malogro
de su primero marido
con el segundo consorcio,
aguardaba en la estacada
el ánimo vigoroso,
que trocó en desfallecido
el ruibarbo y polipodio.
Media noche ora por filo,
y en silencio estaban todos,
cuando el que pensó ser gallo
se halló con fuerzas de pollo.
En bóvedas vedriadas
desató el Ábrigo [*sic*] y Noto,
que en descompuestos boatos
anunciaban terremotos.
Con viva solicitud
tripulaba precuroso [*sic*]
el cuadrado de la cama
por el asiento redondo.
Sentir puede el ver trocadas
quien tuvo de dicha asomos
las glorias de un paraíso
en penas de un purgatorio.
La tristeza le leía
a su consorte en el rostro,
que le paga en vituperios
lo que él pretendió en elogios.
La ostentación de su brío
granjeó por malos modos,
enfado en que asiste mucho
por gusto que dura poco.
Al grado aspiraba de puerco,
con cursos nada olorosos,
quien perdido por ser sabio
hoy gana borla de tonto.
Reniega de quien ha dado
julepe tan enfadoso,
que es causa que lloren cuatro
lo que está purgando un ojo.
A la aurora dio pebetes,
nuevo color a los lodos,
al cuerpo desembarazo
y a cherriones estorbo.

apprehensions to the notice of
others. The bride, with her hopes of
restoring the loss of a first husband
in a second match, was waiting in
the lists for that vigorous
assault . . . which rhubarb and
polypodium were to turn into a very
feeble one. "It was exactly
midnight, and silence reigned over
all" when the cockerel in intention
found himself to be as weak as a
chicken. In glassy vessels he
released the Austral wind and
blustery Notus, the which
foreboded earthquakes in their
uncontrollable plenty. With what
lively alacrity he alternated between
the oblong bed and the circular
close-stool! This bridegroom, who
had secured glimpses of fortune can
now see the glories of paradise
grievously changed into the pains of
purgatory.
Sadness might be read in the face of
his spouse, who rewards with
reproaches the groom who had
expected eulogies.
He chose a most unpleasant means
to show off his physical energy, an
irksome exercise which provides
little pleasure for the movement
involved. He aspired to the degree
of pig, having followed some
malodorous "courses," keen to be
thought so well-trained and now
receiving only the fool's tassel. He
heaps curses on whoever gave him
so noisome a medicine, which has
caused four eyes to weep as much as
one "eye" purged itself of. He cast
perfumes upon the dawn, new
coloration upon the earth, gave
refreshment to his body and extra
work for the nightsoil-carts.

XII-2. AL SUCESO DEL
ENFERMO, CON LA
CONFECCIÓN QUE ESTABA
PARA EL NOVIO.

Un enfermo que desea,
por orden de un esculapio,
purgar humores franchotes
con récipes castellanos,
de una mentirosa purga
pasaba el último trago,
que por gustar de los dulces
hoy prueba de los amargos.
Sentir pudiera a saberlo
de que trate un boticario
a los sanos como a enfermos,
los enfermos como a sanos.
Hizo a su estómago Troya,
y fue el Paladión un vaso,
las cantárides los griegos
y la alteración el daño.
Su sosiego fue la noche,
pero cuando llegó el plazo
secretas armas ostenta
quien guardó silencio tanto.
Poco a poco empieza el fuego
a manifestar estragos
en quien con descuido estuvo
ignorante del engaño.
Ardiendo se esta Troya,
y los entresuelos bajos,
cuando humedades esperan,
llamas están vomitando.
La confusión del incendio
permitió que en gritos altos
manifestasen su injuria
los sentidos ciudadanos.
Curaba de nuestro enfermo
Elena Pérez, regalo
de un venerable deán,
su vecino en otro cuarto,
hembra antigua en quien concurren
unciones, conjuro, ensalmos
y todos los accidentes

WHAT HAPPENED WHEN THE
INVALID SWALLOWED THE
CORDIAL INTENDED FOR THE
BRIDEGROOM

A certain invalid who wished, on the
orders of a physician, to purge
Gallic humors with old Castilian
recipes, swallowed the last drops of
what was falsely termed a purge,
and for his desire to taste sweetness
now instead only experiences
bitterness. He might ponder after
tasting, that an apothecary treats the
healthy as though they were ill, and
the sick as though they were in good
health.
His stomach became Troy in flames;
its Palladium was a drinking glass;
the Greeks invading him were the
cantharides, and the final result was
a real indisposition. Night brought
him some alleviation, but when the
appointed moment came for all his
silence he began to brandish secret
armament. Little by little the fire
begins to produce serious effects in
this unwitting subject of a
deception; he wasn't giving it a
thought.
Troy was now ablaze, the lower story
is belching flames when it shows all
the preparatives for encountering
certain moistnesses.
The fiery confusion prompted his
senses, those citizens of his body's
fortress, to cry aloud about their
deprivation.
A certain Elena Pérez, the
treasured maid of a venerable dean,
tenant of a neighboring apartment,
was in charge of our invalid. This
was an ancient female given to
ointments, conjurations and healing

que piden tres veintes de años.
La cara—que Dios mejore—
recopila en breve espacio
facciones de los que ocupan
de San Antón el retablo.
Mas con todos sus defectos,
el encendido troyano
estas razones le dice,
que por requiebros pasaron:
—Elena, Troya se quema.
por un doctor Menelao
no permitas que perezca
un Paris de matamano.
A tu piedad me encomiendo,
que ponga remedio al daño
de impulsos que siendo duros,
mis ruegos te venzan blandos.
Si entre las acciones frías,
si entre los gustos helados
algún consuelo reservas
para los precisos casos,
sácame del fuego a cuestas
sobre tus miembros ancianos;
que aunque es civil el empleo,
a la hambre no hay pan malo."
La soledad del albergue,
el afecto del malsano,
el fuego que le molesta
y el apretante embarazo
en los pajares de Elena
vivas brasas trasladaron,
que si una casa se enciende
temer pueden las del barrio.
Su piedad ejerce Elena,
y con el joven en brazos
remedia daños del fuego
hasta que le deja en salvo.
De caritativa muestra
su celo, que en atajarlo
las jeringas de la Villa
pienso que no hicieran tanto.

spells, and having all the attributes
attendant usually on threescore
years. Her face—may God improve
it in a future life—assembles in one
reduced area all those features one
expects to find in some picture of
the Temptation of St. Anthony. In
spite of these defects, however, our
fiery Trojan spoke to her thus, in
effect wooing her: "Elena. Troy is
on fire. Don't allow a Paris to perish
pleasuring himself (?) through the
treachery of a medical Menelaus. I
commend myself to your kindness.
Please let my soft supplications
overcome you, and help me remedy
the ill-effects of hard impulses. If,
within your frigid organism, among
your gelid appetites you retain some
capacity to console desperate cases,
carry me out of the flames on your
ancient limbs.
Although the task is a brutal one,
hunger knows no stale bread." The
solitude of that dwelling, the ardor
of the invalid, the inflammation
causing his discomfort and the
urgency of the occasion, all sent
living flames into the thatch of
Elena, for if one house catches fire,
all those in the vicinity may also fear
it. Elena shows her sympathy in
practical fashion, and with the
young man in her arms she takes
away all the ill-effects of the blaze
until he is safe and sound. She
shows such zeal in her charitable
assignment that I doubt very much
whether all the syringes of Madrid
could have done equally well.

XIII. A UNA DAMA QUE
DORMIA, Y UN MONO PARTÍA

ON A LADY WHO FELL
ASLEEP, WHILE A MONKEY

PIÑONES Y COMÍA JUNTO A ELLA.

SPLIT AND ATE PINENUTS BY HER SIDE

Parias tributa a Morfeo,
deidad que cruel permite
a suma beldad desmayos,
a claro esplendor eclipses;
mortífera acción obstenta [*sic*],
si bien aún lo hermoso vive
con orfandad de dos soles,
cuyos fulgores extingue—
que vuelto en nuestra vulgata,
cuando más se descultice,
querrá decir todo junto
que estaba durmiendo Filis.
Temerosa en el verano
de la pensión de las chinches,
que sin jugar a los cientos
a cada instante dan piques,
escoge para la siesta,
cuando el Can celeste gime
y la chicharra vocea,
tarima, estera y cojines.
Avarienta de su vista
pretende que se retire,
y escudriñando intestinos
es de su estómago lince.
En tanto pues que soñaba
empleos de sus melindres
en el zaguán de su idea
si no palpables, visibles,
un remedo de los hombres,
un epítome risible,
sagaz, si animal, que dio
oficio a los boratines:
un mono, por no deciros
palabras por alambiques,
escolta hace a su dueño,
doméstico como humilde,
si bien su entretenimiento,
goloso cuanto apacible,
era comer de la fruta
de quien Atis fue su origen.[11]

She renders tribute to Morpheus,
that cruel deity who ordains
unconsciousness for the greatest
beauties, eclipses in the fairest
radiances; who exhibits
death-dealing capabilities, albeit
beauty is still alive though orphaned
of the two suns whose brilliance he
has put out. All of which, translated
into our vernacular and entirely
"decultified," can mean in short that
Phyllis lay asleep.
Apprehensive of the bedbugs, a
plague in summer which, though
not playing at "hundreds," "score
points" every time, she selects for
her siesta, while the Dog Star
whimpers and the cicada shrills, a
mat, a rug and some cushions.
Jealous of being oberved, she
retires, and turning her gaze
inward, she becomes the lynx of her
own inner self.
While she was dreaming, passing
through the forecourt of her mental
world possible future applications
for her cajoleries—visualized if not
palpable—a little imitation man, a
ludicrous scale-model, sagacious
though merely an animal, who had
helped some mountebanks to gain a
living (that is, a monkey; need I
distill my words in alembics?) was at
this moment the companion of his
mistress, docile and tame.
His amusement, however, was to
nibble at that fruit which originated
with the metamorphosis of Attis.
With a natural lasciviousness, with
an inviting object before him and

Con lascivo natural,
con objeto apetecible,
y con piñones por pasto,
¿quién habrá que se averigüe?
Disculparle quiero al mono,
que con la fruta y el brindis
no era mucho acumular
incentivos varoniles.
Mal puede hacer la razón,
que sus impulsos corrigen
ligaduras de metal
que a los cautivos oprime.
¡Cuánto diera por traer
en ocasión tan felice
la fuerte insignia que dio
a los Mazas noble timbre!
Culpa se tuvo la dama
en el casero combite,
que en cada piñón sus ganas
cobran filos más sutiles.
¡Guárdate, Filis! ¡Despierta!
Que si atropella imposibles
te espera una tarquinada,
si no es gozo de Pasife;
que si en la tal calabriada
inadvertida concibes,
nos darás un filimono
por esos bajos países.

with pinenuts as a stimulant, who is
there who might be sure of himself?
I incline toward excusing the
monkey, for with the dessert and
the open invitation it was no wonder
that he should soon feel the
promptings of his virility. Reason
can hardly come into play here, but
his desires are held in check by
shackles of that metal which
captives are laden with. How much
would he give if someone would
bring him, on this lucky occasion, a
hammer, that powerful emblem
used as a device by the Maza clan!
The lady was at fault at this
houseparty; after all, each bite into a
pinenut only set a keener edge on
the simian lust.
Beware, Phyllis! Wake up! Because
if he should manage to get past his
restraints you will surely be taken
violently, pleasured as Pasiphae
was. If as a result of such a
commingling you should
inadvertently become impregnated,
you will present us with a
Phyllipithecus from those nether
regions.

XIV. [EL AMOR LAPIDARIO]

LOVE AMONG THE GEMSTONES.

Pascual, si por tu mujer
a lapidario te inclinas,
de tratar en cornerinas
topacio vendrás a ser.[12]

Pascual, if you, at the instance of
your wife, take up the collecting of
precious stones, remember that if
you deal in cornalines you will end
by being a topaz.

Si tu mujer halla en ti,
Pascual, un buen ayudante,
sin dejar a don Diamante
gozará a mosén Rubí.
Cada cual gane por sí,
y tú harás por lo advertido

If your wife, Pascual, finds you to be
a good assistant in her plans,
without neglecting Sir Diamond she
will take her pleasure with Sir
Ruby. Let each look out for himself,
and you will affect, now that you are

disimulos de marido,
y orejas de mercader.
Pascual, si por tu mujer, &c.

*

Quien piedras quiere juntar
con don Julio y don Lope,
es fuerza las halle al tope,
que es amigo de topar.
Tú la puedes imitar,
aunque en modo diferente,
quien de tres signos pariente
tan cercano viene a ser.
Pascual, si por tu mujer, &c.

XV. [REMIGIO, HIDALGO
FAMÉLICO]

Plinio, el que tantas patrañas
escribió en lo natural—
que a ser escritor de a legua
él se moderara más—
dice que naturaleza
fue con el oso voraz
avara, pues en invierno
alimentos no le da,
porque quiere que le sirva
su propio humor de manjar,
y que con él se sustente
como si fuera truhan.
Consigo trae el consuelo
la mano en el paladar,
como el hueso de tocino
el borgoñón o alemán,
hasta que en la primavera
salir pueda a campear
y a escalar casas de abejas
por lo dulce del panal.
Tal le sucede a Remigio,
un hidalgo de solar
que fue asilo de parientes,
y de los grajos lo es ya.

aware of this, a husband's discretion
and ears that do not hear.

She who wishes to put together a
stone collection with Don Julio and
Don Lope of necessity will assay
them by direct contact. He's well
acquainted with such encounters.
You may imitate her, though not
quite in the same way: you have
collected as your close relatives the
three horned signs of the zodiac,
Taurus, Aries and Capricorn.

REMIGIO, A PAUPER *HIDALGO*

Pliny, he who spun so many yarns
about natural history—for if he'd
been some miscellaneous writer he
would have moderated what he
said—observes that Nature was
niggardly towards the hungry bear,
providing him with no food in the
winter and expecting him to make
his meals out of his own juices. Like
a "man of humor" he must keep
alive on these.
He carries with him his consolation
in the paw he holds in his mouth,
rather like a Burgundian or a
German sucking on a hambone,
until in the spring he can go out for a
stroll and rob the bees' homes for
sweet honeycombs.
The same thing happens with
Remigio, a landed gentleman who
was once the refuge of his relatives;
now only jackdaws are his
companions. Such an honorable
man of substance that he has never

Tan honrado hombre de bien
que ha disimulado el mal
que con su cara de hereje[13]
le da la necesidad.
El ya caduco vestido
con más tramoyas está
que los carros de la Corte
en fiesta sacramental.
Los zapatos colorados
de puro corridos van,
publicando su pobreza
con lenguas de Fregenal.
Diole el cielo desenfado
con esta calamidad,
tanto, que a quien conoce
da ocasión para enfadar.
Es hombre que por su olfato
a un banquete se hallará,
aunque se haga en una cueva,
aunque se haga en un desván.
Siempre fue del mediodía
comilitón puntual,
tanto que la contumacia
no se la dieron jamás.
De limpiarse a servilleta
nunca cuidadoso va,
que en él viene a ser provecho
lo que en otros suciedad,
porque las más de las noches
pasa con cena mental,
y en el olor de sus dedos
libranzas al hambre da.
Este huésped os espera;
líbrese dél cada cual,
que va ligero a la presa
como hambriento gavilán.

allowed the hard luck which
necessity, with its heretic's face, has
inflicted on him, to show. His
worn-out clothes have more pieces
of rigging than the Corpus Christi
pageant carts of Madrid. His shoes
go blushing red out of pure shame,
declaring his poverty with their
tongues of Fregenal leather.
Heaven endowed him with a
carefree nature in the midst of this
chaotic life, so much so that he
causes irritation to all his
acquaintances. He is a man who can
find his way to a dinner by his sense
of smell, even though it is being
served in a cellar or a garret.
He was ever a punctual companion
at the midday meal, so much so that
he has never been given the slip in
time by the diners.
He has no interest in wiping himself
clean with his napkin, because what
in others would be thought
slovenliness is in him thrift. Most
evenings he is content with a supper
consumed in the mind only, and he
relieves his hunger with a whiff from
his fingers.
This guest, then awaits you. May
everyone avoid meeting him, for he,
like a famished falcon, is swift after
his prey.

XVI. [REMIGIO] EN RESPUESTA DEL PASADO.

Non es de sesudos homes,
nin de infanzones de pro,
el escarnir de un fidalgo

REMIGIO MAKES REPLY

It does no honor to intelligent
wights nor to worthy gentry to mock
at a nobleman with the impudence

con denuesto trobador.
Maguer poco ataviado,
finca del solar mejor
que el sol fermoso remira
del dorado carretón.
Non los rotos atavíos
quitan las vertudes, non,
que natura en el fidalgo
con engrudo las pegó.
Claraboyado el bohemio
su valor descobijó,
que non perjodica el tiempo,
siendo él claraboyador.
Desempuntadas las calzas
de lo que aguja tejió,
non desempuntan su ingenio
nin desfacen su primor.
Desfarrapados zapatos,
de cordobán sin color,
non le dan malo a la fama
que de buena non torció.
E si fambriento os semeja
por yantar de mogollón,
necessitas caret lege:
cara de hereje y peor.
Escondriñar un combite
fácelo todo oledor,
quier se siente combidado,
quier non le den refación.
Talante amuesa Remigio
además de yantador,
mas non es tan foribundo
cual debujan al león.
Non al oso glotonazo
le dedes comparación,
que él es animal peloso;
a éste pelo no cobrió.
Si porque partido el tiempo
de cenas non se pagó,
non apliquedes que yace
sosteniéndose de humor,
que, para Santa María,
que tengo por sandio yo
al que fiebres solecita

of some minstrel. Maugre his
unseemly port, his stock is of the
comeliest demesne that the fair sun
beholds from his gilded wain.
Torn raiment abates not the virtues,
no indeed, for Dame Nature herself
fixed them with glue into the
hidalgo.
His short cloak, with its skylights,
leaves his worthiness unconcealed,
but time puts that worthiness in no
hazard. Time is the piercer of all
things. Though his trunkhose be
coming apart from the seams
wrought by the needle, his wit does
not therefore come apart, nor is his
excellence to-broken on that
account. Down-at-heel shoon, their
uppers discolored, impair not the
good name of him who never
deserved aught but the good. And if
he seems famished when he feasts,
well, necessity knows no law, with
her heretic's visage and worse.
Inquiring into a dining party is what
every wight with a nose does, an he
sit down invited or be unfeasted.
Remigio reveals a talent for more
than being a frequenter of banquets,
but the lion is not so fierce as they
draw him.
Compare him not with the
gluttonous bear, for your bear is a
hairy beast, and Remigio had never
hairy weed to cover himself with.
If, as time went by, he could never
stay himself with dinners, aver not
that he now lies ingesting his own
corporeal humors, for by Our Lady,
I reckon as a wittol that wight who
becomes stricken of the fever
through his craving for good fare.
There is no wisdom in one who is
seduced by his yearning for the

por la fucia de glotón;
que non es sabeduría
por mañas de golosmión
yacer doliente en el lecho,
pescudar por el doctor
e denpués que es ya venido,
e la moñeca tomó,
encaminallo a la muerte
con brebajes de rigor.
Oso sea, y muy osado,
nueso Remigio garzón,
porque sus fijos non den
dinero al sepultador.
Yante en la metad del día
a su talante e sabor,
e diga lo que quijere
el escarnidor fisgón.

delights of the table, lying suffering
in bed and sending for the
physician; and when he has arrived
and taken his pulse, letting him
speed him on his way to death with
ruthless draughts.
In his boldness, yes, let our worthy
Remigio be a bear, so that his
children may need to give no money
to the gravedigger.
May he dine in the midday in his
own fashion and at his ease, and let
the losel gossips have their say as
they will.

XVII. EL ROBO DE EUROPA

THE ABDUCTION OF EUROPA

Protocoro famoso,
que en el luciente carril
iluminas doce casas,
sin dejar zaquizamí—
que te fueran provechosas
a tenerlas en Madrid,
en el golfo donde surca
todo coche bergantín—
a una de tus nueve hermanas,
la de ingenio más feliz,
le pido que de Castalia
me traiga lleno un barril,
porque penetre la historia,
con vista de zahorí,
de aquella Dama robada
del Toro, ladrón sutil.
Hubo Agenor, rey fenicio,
en cualquier amorosa lid—
si las de los matrimonios
se pueden llamar así—
una hija hermosa y bella,
por lo cándido marfil,
por lo rubio oro del Tíbar,[14]
clavel por lo carmesí.

Matchless precentor, you who in
the shining pathway illuminate
twelve houses, not omitting a single
attic (and it would be profitable for
you to have those houses situated in
Madrid, in that gulf where every
brigantine of a coach is under weigh)
I ask that one of your Nine Sisters,
the one with the most sparkling wit,
may bring me a full cask from
Castalia, so that I may penetrate
with a diviner's eye, the story of that
Lady who was stolen away by a
subtle thief of a Bull.
Now Agenor, King of Phoenicia, in
one of the jousts of love—if those
within the limits of matrimony may
be so styled—begot a beautiful
daughter, like ivory in her
whiteness, with the gold of Tíbar in
her hair, and having the complexion
of a carnation. As usual in a woman,
she was of a flighty disposition and,
without ever actually treading the

Esta fue mujer al uso,
de espíritu volatín,
que sin andar por maroma
dicen que fue saltatriz.
Salíase por los campos
con el gremio femenil,
que eran las cubicularias
que la asisten a servir.
Embidiosas las dejaba
su donaire y gracias mil,
que era en estremo perfeta
del copete al escarpín.
Yendo y viniéndose días,
según estilo civil,
en uno el Rey de los Dioses
abrió un cancel de zafir.
Vio la moza más bizarra
que vestido [*sic*] caniquí
desde el pobre Manzanares
al rico Guadalquivir.
Andaba entonces Cupido
más suelto que un arlequín,
preciando más captivarle
que a cuatro maravedís.
Dorado harpón
le dispara
con fuerza más que pueril,
dejándole por Europa
vuelto de dios, matachín.
Cosquillas siente en el alma,
sin poderse resistir,
que la comezón de amor
es peor que de arastín.
Mil trazas para gozarla
fabrica allá en su magín,
más que en planta de una casa
arquitecto o albañir.
Transformose el Dios Tonante
en el toro más cerril
que han visto los verdes campos
pacer, escarbar, mugir.
La piel que cubre su cuerpo
no es armino [*sic*] baladí,
porque con la misma nieve puede

tightrope, made her leaps, so they
say. She would go out into the fields
with her female companions, that is,
the maids-in-waiting who helped in
serving her, and she left them all
envious with her wit and her
thousand graces.
She was perfect in the extreme,
from her topknot down to her shoes.
As the days came and went,
according to their customary style,
one morning the monarch of the
gods opened a skylight of sapphire,
and glimpsed the most ravishing lass
to wear muslin between the
indigent Manzanares and the
opulent Guadalquivir.
Cupid was at that time running
about with the agility of a
Harlequin, and was keener on
bagging Jupiter than four farthings.
He fires off a golden harpoon at him,
with more than boyish alacrity,
leaving the god dwindled into a
puppet, no more. He notices the
ticklings within his very soul,
unable to resist, for the itch of love
is worse than that of crablice (?). In
his imagination he constructs a
thousand plans, for her conquest,
more than an architect or a builder
makes for a house.
The God of Thunder transformed
himself into the wildest bull that has
ever been seen to graze, stamp and
bellow in the fields. The hide which
covers his form is not like ordinary
ermine, rather it may be compared
with snow itself.
The lovely lady had hardly sighted
the noble animal, evidently a
friendly one, though astute in his
approach, when she arrived with
her ladies where he was. She ended

muy bien competir.
Apenas la hermosa dama
vio el animal tan gentil,
en lo aparente agradable
cuanto astuto en el fingir,
cuando llegó con sus damas,
perdido el temor al fin,
que el ver toros cada instante
puede el miedo divertir.
Doméstico, si brioso,
viene a presentarse allí
a quien presumió fierezas,
según el buen discurrir.
Entre damas y mondongas,
espantadizas de un tris,
para asegurarlas más
hizo la yerba cojín.
Perdido el temor al toro,
de la rosa, del jazmín,
de la retama y junquillo,
la violeta y alelí
le forman varias guirnaldas,
y la armazón tan feliz—
que ha sido timbre de tantos—
adornan con flores mil.
Agradecido y amable
dio causa en estarlo así
que doncellas caballonas
en él quisiesen subir.
Hubo algunas marimachos
de quien la infanta aprendiz
oprimió el cándido lomo,
agarrándose a la crin.
Mas apenas siente el Toro
a quien desea sentir,
cuando de carrera parte
a ser en el mar delfín.
Al Dios Marino invocaba
que le permita salir
del districto de su imperio,
para conseguir su fin.
Tendió el tridente Neptuno
en el salado viril,
y allanando crespas olas

by losing all fear, because the
frequent sight of bulls can overcome
fear of them in anyone.
He steps forward to introduce
himself, tame though fiery, to a lady
who might easily have presumed
him to be ferocious, following the
best authorities. Since he is now
among easily frightened ladies—and
their "innards"—he makes the grass
into a cushion, to reassure them.
Once they have lost their fear of the
bull they make many garlands—of
the rose, the jasmine, the broom,
the gladiolus, the violet and the
gillyflower—and in carefree fashion
adorn his horns (which have served
as an emblem to so many) with a
thousand flowers. In his gratitude
and amiability he allowed maidens
to clamber like horsewomen on to
his back.
There were tomboys among them,
from whom the princess learned
how to settle herself on the
glistening back of the bull, holding
on to his mane. But scarcely had the
bull felt the one is really desired to
be mounted there, than he galloped
off into the sea, moving through the
water like a dolphin. He cried out to
the Sea-God to let him leave the
purlieus of his realm, to bring off his
plan.
Then Neptune held forth his trident
over that salty mirror, and
smoothing the surging waves he
allowed them to get to shore. The
pseudo-bovine god brings to land in
this way his terrified lady, hoping
that fears occasioned by this
grievous theft had not caused her to
soil herself. He has an equal fear of
the anxieties which might afflict her

les dio lugar a surgir.
Pasa el taurífice dios
la dama asustado así,
temiendo no la corrompan
miedos del robo infeliz.
Tanto teme las congojas
que la pueden afligir
como que la piel le manche
con mascado perejil.
Llegó a la opuesta ribera,
descompuesto el faldellín,
y con el temor perdido
un coturno, o un chapín.
A su primer [*sic*] forma vuelve
el que no ocupó toril,
cobrando en verle la dama
nuevo esmalte de carmín.
Con amorosos requiebros
la quiere obligar allí,
si antes la ofenden agravios
de su cauteloso ardid.
Entráronse a un bosquecillo,
a quien el florido abril
hizo opaco con las plantas
del olmo y del tamariz.
La nunca pisada yerba,
el cantueso, el torongil,
por hacer ameno el suelo
le dio vistoso telliz.
No digo lo que pasaron;
dígalo Ovidio por mí,
que anduvo largo en su historia
como lo fue de nariz.

and the stain from "chewed parsley"
which could stain his hide.
She arrived on the opposite shore
with her petticoat disarrayed and, as
a result of the shock, without one of
her buskins (or perhaps her
chopines). This god who had never
occupied a bull's stall reassumes his
original shape, and his lady, seeing
him now, blushes rosily all anew.
With loving words he seeks to
seduce her there and then, although
a moment before the brusqueness of
his wily stratagem had put her off.
They entered a little copse, which
April made impenetrable to the
light with boughs of elm and
tamarisk. The untrodden grass, the
lavender and the balsam provided a
showy covering and made the
ground more pleasurable still.
I shall not describe what they did
there. Let Ovidius Naso say it for
me, for he was as long in telling his
version of the tale as he was long in
the nose.

XVIII. DE UN AMIGO A QUIEN
CONVIDÓ EL AUTOR PARA LA
ACADEMIA UNA NOCHE DE
INVIERNO.

FROM A FRIEND WHOM THE
AUTHOR HAD INVITED TO
THE ACADEMY ONE WINTER
NIGHT

Señor secretario, anoche
ir no pude a la academia,
que nieve y lodos obligan

Dear secretary, I was unable to get
to the academy last night, because
snow and mire force one to do what

a lo que el hombre no piensa.
fuime a ver de una hermosura
los extremos, que lo fueran
a haber menos que lo digan
ya que hay tantos que lo sepan.
Es la mujer agradable,
cuyas ventanas y puertas
jamás sufrieron porfías
y nunca escucharon quejas.
Dase a todos muy barata,
aunque muy cara les cuesta;
y si no es por lo que dan
viene a ser por lo que llevan.
Mas si por la variedad
es naturaleza bella,
en su hermosura es Lisarda
la misma naturaleza.
Teniendo tantos, no tiene
hombre que le favorezca,
y así de lo que le sobra
le falta lo que desea.
Por armas tiene un botín
con una ingeniosa letra,
que dice en lengua vulgar:
"Alejandro de sí mesma".[15]
Con ésta fui flaco anoche;
fuerte fui anoche con ésta,
que el valor en la caída
fue más que en la residencia.
Y después de levantado
volví a caer en la cuenta
de que se pasó la causa
del daño que se recela.
Al fin, como condenado
dando gracias por ofensas,
pagué de mi propia bolsa
a mi verdugo mi afrenta.
Esta noche no he dormido,
llorando mis desdichas,
pensando en lo que pasó
y temiendo lo que queda.
Rogad, amigo, a los cielos,
si os oyen sus luces bellas,
que mi temor sea por bien,

one hadn't hoped to. I went to
admire the charms of a certain
beauty, which would indeed be
charms if there were fewer to
describe them—but there are so
many who are familiar with the
subject. She's an agreeable woman,
whose windows and doors have
never held out against importunities
nor listened to lovers' plaints. She
gives herself quite cheaply to every
man, though she can be very
expensive: not so much for what
they bring, but in what they carry
away. If it's true that Nature is
beautiful because of her very
variousness, then Lisarda is nature
herself in beauty. She is no man's
favorite, though she possesses so
many, and therefore she goes short
amid plenty of what she most could
care to have. Her emblem is a
slipper, together with an ingenious
motto: "An Alexander in her
generosity with her own self." Last
night I surrendered to moral
weakness with this woman; also I
tested my strength with her last
night, because I showed more
fortitude in my moment of debility
than what followed it. After I had
once again pulled myself together I
realized that the reason for that
much feared weakness of will was no
longer valid. Like some condemned
criminal making his atonement for
wrongs he has done I paid my own
executioner, out of my own purse,
for this infamy. Last night I could
not sleep as I bewept my moment of
prowess, reflecting on what
happened and fearing developments
yet to come. Pray, my friend, to
heaven, if you have any influence

o por menos mal siquiera;
y que de tan grave culpa
se me dé la penitencia,
ya que pecó la carne,
sin que los huesos lo sientan.
Y pues la imaginación
en los tristes atormenta
aun con afectos fingidos
como las verdades mesmas;
ya que padezco en la mía,
pudiendo tener mis penas
remedios de vuestras manos,
no es justo que así padezca.
Respondedme y consoladme,
que por mi desdicha crea
que, en sus extremos mayores,
no hay mal que por bien no venga.

with its shining luminaries, that my
fears may have a happy ending, or at
least the least unhappy one, and
that I may atone for this grave fault
without my bones contracting a
lasting ill, when only the flesh
sinned. And since the imagination
torments the afflicted as much with
fancied griefs as with real ones, it
isn't fair that my imagination should
be in torment when I know that
your own hands hold the remedy.
Answer me and console me, that I
may come to believe through my
own misfortune that, even in the
most extreme situations, there's no
evil that doesn't come for one's
good.

XIX. RESPUESTA.

Disculpa el obedeceros
el que en escribir delincue,
a versos que son tan doctos
con ignorancias humildes.
No todos usan discretos
del sacro humor de Aganipe;
pues su pilón ya es patente
a caballos y rocines.
En el cuartago lenguaje
que mi musa me permite—
porque quien más no merece
no ha de pedir imposibles—
os digo, señor amigo,
que vuestro ingenio felice
hizo falta en la academia
del claro desdén de Clicie,
si bien estáis disculpado
con el rigor insufrible
de la nieve y vendaval,
que una hiela y otro gime.
Mas quien con tanto calor
busca Lamias, busca Circes,
pudiera pasar los Puertos

REPLY

Forgive one who is guilty of
scribbling insignificant and uncouth
verses in reply to your most expert
ones.
Not everybody is prudent in the
draughts he takes from the fount of
Aganippe; too many use the
drinking trough open to horses and
hacks.
In that language—but a few hands
high—that my Muse allows me (and
one who does not deserve better
should not ask for the impossible) I
shall explain to you, my friend, that
your apt repartee was sadly missed
in the literary gathering dedicated
to Apollo, that shining god who
disdained Clytie. You are forgiven,
though, on account of the
unbearable force of the snow and
the storm, as they freeze and moan
aloud. But someone who has such
heat contained within himself as to

de Guadarrama y Bembibre.
Por la vista relación
hallo que gozar quisistes
empleo de ropería
adonde todos se visten.
En mesón de variedad
donde huéspedes se admiten
siempre es patente la estafa,
y siempre expulso el melindre.
Detenidos pretendientes
adonde quejas publiquen
son embarazos de calles
por quien vecinos registren.
Menos escándalo causan
seis ocultos albañires,
dándoles barro a la mano,
que no un público cacique.
Hizo bien la tal señora
no hacerse huraña y difícil,
que en estos tiempos modernos
la que huye no se sigue.
Suelen estas mancebías
con brevedad remitirse
a galicias experiencias,
y no se ignora el origen.
Todo venéreo bajel,
y el timonero que rige,
debe temer el escollo
y guardarse de la Sirte.
El vuestro, que anda surcando
mares de varios países,
para conocer bajíos
le conviene ser un lince,
que en este mar de Madrid
hay sirenas contra Ulises,
sin que la cera les valga
para que su encanto eviten.
Hay harpías que a las otras
les pueden dar falta y quince,
de quien no hay presas que
emboten uñas que son tan sutiles.
Hay . . . mas ceso porque os canso;
y a esto podréis decirme
que al fin no hay cuerdo a caballo,

go seeking Lamias and Circes
should easily be able to survive the
Passes of Guadarrama and
Bembibre. From the account I have
seen I notice that you wanted to
amuse yourself trying on clothes in a
shop where every man finds
something to wear. In a place of
varied merchandise where guests
are catered for, cheating is always
on the cards and shows of affection
are always out of place. Wherever
lovers station themselves in public
places to make their plaints, they
become an obstruction observed by
the dwellers nearby. Six
bricklayers, once they have their
material, cause less scandal,
provided they work in private, than
one prominent person in public.
The lady in question did well in not
making herself evasive or difficult,
because in these days she who runs
away will not be pursued. These
associations frequently transform
themselves into encounters with the
morbus Gallicus, and the cause of it
all comes to light. The helmsman of
every amorous craft must be wary of
the hidden shoal and avoid the
sandbank. Your own craft, then,
which navigates through the waters
of many lands needs a very lynx for a
helmsman, to spy out the sandspits.
In this ocean of Madrid the sirens
are out to get the Ulysseses, and
wax is of no use against their
charms. Harpies there are who can
win every trick against those of
Antiquity; no prey can blunt their
exquisite claws.
There are . . . but I'll end here, as I
exhaust you. You may reply that just
as no man is in his wits when he's on

ni hombre continente a un brindis.
Y si esto es ansí, os le hago
y os convido a varios chistes
en la futura academia,
pues la pasada no fuistes.

horseback, so there is no abstemious
man in the face of an open
invitation. If this is so, I send you
my open invitation: to a variety of
witty moments in the academy in
times to come—seeing that you
missed the last session.

XX. A LA FIESTA DE SANTIAGO EL VERDE EN EL SOTILLO DE MANZANARES DE MADRID.

THE FIESTA OF SANTIAGO EL VERDE IN THE SOTILLO DE MANZANARES, MADRID

Sus armazones jugaba
contra Castor, contra Pólux,
porque presentan al mayo
el ya tripulado Toro,
cuando la señora Corte,
mucho a mucho y poco a poco,
vomitaba sabandijas
que trasladaba en un Soto.
Una escuadra de galeras
parecían yendo en corso:
los coches que van sulcando
ya por barro y ya por polvo.
Cada galera terrestre,
en día tan venturoso,
solía ser un serrallo,
o archivo de monipodios,
cuya desorden el tiempo
puso límite y estorbo,
entibiando el donativo
los temores de algún soplo.
¡Qué trotón, haca o rocín
no buscaron cuidadosos,
en que hacerse caballeros
don Camilo y don Leopoldo!
Salieron desafuciados
de corbetas y corcovos,
con dos largos mondadientes
tan vírgines [*sic*] como ociosos.

The Bull, already caparisoned, was
trying out his armament against
Castor and Pollux, when they were
offering him to May, when Lady
Madrid was expelling her creatures,
either little by little or in volume,
and conveying them to the Soto.
A squadron of terrestrial galleys
appeared, on patrol; these were
coaches, under weigh either
through mud or through dust. Each
of these galleys of the streets, on so
pleasant a day, was customarily a
seraglio in itself, or perhaps a coven
of rogues, to the licentiousness of
which time put a limit and an
obstacle. Fears of tattling tongues
cooled down the drivers' generosity.
How Don Camilo and Don
Leopoldo carefully sought out
trotting-horses, hacks and nags, to
present themselves as cavaliers!
They set out—on their last
legs—with curvets—and their bent
backs—holding what seemed to be
two long, useless (and unused)
toothpicks. Doña Blanca and Doña
Tecla, maidens of the order of the

Doña Blanca y doña Tecla,[16]
doncellas del Tusón de Oro,
una sale a ocupar bolsas
y otra a tocarse de todos.
Quien tuvo esperanza coche
cubrió a un sardesco los lomos,
y en la posesión jamuga
se desvaneció su toldo.
Doña Sara y doña Eva,
con embarnizados rostros,
desmienten ancianidades
haciendo melindres mozos.
Con los huéspedes se alegra,
más altivo que brioso,
el enano de los ríos,
gigante de los arroyos.
Vadeábanle sirenas,
cuando en su menguado golfo
alguna cara de plata   ⅃
mostró sus piernas de plomo.
¡Qué de bailes, qué de juegos,
qué de fiestas y alborozo
ostentaba el Soto alegre
para empleo de los ojos!
En los cándidos manteles
los estómagos golosos
a Ceres con Baco juntan
en merendable consorcio.
Los brindis menudeaban
los bacanales pilotos,
sin que a bota o a garrafa
les dejan un trago solo.
No se mostró ocioso Marte,
que entre lo alegre y yocoso
hubo danzantes de espada,
sin ser la fiesta del Corpus.
Cansose el señor de Delo—
aliás el dios Apolo—
y por holgarse con Tetis
dejó el carro luminoso.
Todos vuelven a Madrid,
dejándome algo dudoso
si siendo la gente tanta
habrá camas para todos.

* * * * * *

Golden Fleece, also set out, the one
to insinuate herself into purses, the
other to touch every note. He who
had a coach only in his mind's
aspirations covered the back of his
donkey, and transformed a
stall-covering into asinine trappings.
Doña Sara and Doña Eva, their
faces varnished, hide their ancient
selves beneath the youthful gestures
they affect. Manzanares, that dwarf
among rivers and giant among
brooks, more presumptuous than
animated, enjoys himself amid the
pleasure-party. Sirens waded in his
waters, and lower down than their
silver faces could be seen reflected
their base metal legs. What dances,
what games, what festivity and
tumult did the happy Soto have to
show for the delight of the eyes! On
white tablecloths keen stomachs
join Ceres to Bacchus in lunchtime
matrimony.
The toastmasters, pilots of the
bacchanal, multiplied their
offerings, and left not a single
mouthful in bottle or flask. Mars was
not lazy either, for amid the playful
throng there could be seen
sword-dancers, even though this
was not Corpus Christi—The Lord of
Delos, otherwise known as Apollo,
tired himself out and left the radiant
chariot to disport himself with
Thetis. Back they all go to Madrid,
leaving me in some perplexity: with
so many folk, will there be a bed for
every one?

* * * * * *

CHAPTER 8

Conclusion

A LONSO de Castillo Solórzano's works stand as a particularly elegant record of the penetration of the novella form and of the story of pilgrimage and adversity by structures of feeling and incident which have always meant much to the unreflective reader of fiction. Far from registering a decline in specifically literary quality or in alertness to the human situation from the moment of Cervantes's *Exemplary Novels,* Castillo's fictions bear witness to the permanence of the elements of romance, of "purveyed literature." The undemanding reader will always find an appeal in accounts of the fulfillment of romantic desires, in love and in fortune, amid scenery and in circumstances more captivating than his or her own. So it is that we should not speak of a decline but of one of the more striking resumptions of whatever vivacity may be found in the Italian novella collections and the "Byzantine" novels of the century preceding Castillo's. If we decide to look at Castillo's fictions in this way we might also concede that the tabulation and analysis of his many fictional plots become of minor importance, and that the thing to isolate is perhaps the congeries of fictional structures which are indices of psychic tensions in the society to which he had his readers belonged. One example of such a structure is the representation of a "Don Juan" figure in action, which Castillo's play *Outrage Atoned For* illustrates so clearly. It may well be that Don Juan was not the unique creation of Tirso de Molina but rather, objectivized a tension sensed by several dramatists of a given epoch, the seventeenth century.

The name of Castillo Solórzano will, however, be inseparable for most readers of our day from his longer novels of rogues and pranksters, usually attached on superficial grounds to the corpus of Spanish picaresque novels. The study of these works has always left some perplexity in the minds of investigators, who frequently went

117

on to discover in them, unconvincingly, "realistic pictures of society," manners and customs of lovable rogues and pert wenches or, in more serious vein, evidence of the social malaise of urban Spain in Castillo's century. This was probably inevitable when one considers that these works were most translated and adapted, into English especially, at a time—the early eighteenth century—when such discoveries were sought after in "purveyed literature." Books about highwaymen eagerly read in Queen Anne's London and the scandalous revelations of Mrs. Manley and Mrs. Hayward have in fact interposed themselves, and we have to go back to Castillo's own pieces. We have proposed that *The Girl-Trickster, The She-Stoat* and the rest should be read as relations about characters "of quality," from which these latter are accidentally absent. The unprincipled companions of ladies and gentlemen "of quality" in these cases take over the theater of activity. Castillo, it has often been re- marked, never actually shows this lack of principle being punished but always promises to do so "in the sequel." We might speculate that his scheme of values cannot accommodate such punishment, since these swindling and mocking characters are, for all their elab- oration, not drawn from the world of human beings at all but from that of the *figurae* of farce, detached from the moral order.

Castillo, then, makes his fictional appeal to a wide spectrum of desires and impulses in the unreflective mass of consumers of fiction, from wishes for love and adventure in idealized cir- cumstances, through vicarious, even snobbish indulgence in the enjoyment of sumptuous interiors and conspicuous promenades, to the ignoble tyranny of those who were loyal to "normal" social val- ues over those others who were considered deviant and unaccepta- ble by people "of quality". Farce surely possesses this root in feel- ings of social decorum as well as another in cruel and irrational human psychic impulses.

This brings us to the assessment of Castillo's strengths as an au- thor: the many occasions when the reader has to applaud him even while he admits that our author is degrading the nature of men and women almost beyond recognition. His *figurones*, the buffoon characters which he developed, seem to have gone on to fortune. The connection of such characters with the humorists found in eighteenth century works (and in the eighteenth century sense of the word "humorist") is not so clearly established but may well eventually lead to another small glory reflected upon Castillo as an innovator. Perhaps the most neglected area of Castillo's work, and one which would repay investigation, is his poetry, including here the more sustained speeches by *graciosos* in his plays and *figuras* in his interludes. We have to acclaim his unfailing agility and diligently pruned diction in his whole production of unserious verse.

Notes and References

Chapter One

1. Bennassar, Bartolomé. *Valladolid au Siècle d'or* (Paris and The Hague: Mouton, 1967).

2. *Ibid.*, 237–8.

3. King, Willard F. *Prosa novelística y academias literarias en el siglo XVII* (Madrid: Real Academia Española, 1963), 53. This work is by far the most useful for our understanding of Castillo and the forces active in the literary world of his time in Madrid, and also, 211 *et seq.*, of the close interdependence of literary societies and the fiction-writers' technique of narrating stories within stories during the years 1620–1635. Professor King produces interesting evidence of social aspects of these societies: how rich members would buy compositions from indigent poets and read them out as their own work (138), and how ladies would participate, although wearing veils, in these meetings *"por acreditarse de buenos gustos"* ("to gain a reputation for being persons of taste") (page 167).

4. I use this term in accordance with the arguments of Gerald Gillespie in his article "Novella, Nouvelle, Novelle, Short Novel? A Review of Terms", *Neophilologus*, 51 (1967), 117–27 and 225–30. His conclusion (p. 230, note 16) is that "The best expression for English is probably the Italian form, ... [that is, *novella*]."

5. Yudin, Florence L. "The *Novela corta* as *Comedia*. Lope's *Las fortunas de Diana*," *Bulletin of Hispanic Studies* 45 (1968), 181–88, and "Theory and Practice of the *Novela comediesca*," *Romanische Forschungen*, 81 (1969), 585–94.

6. Hints as to some other obstacles encountered by Castillo in his fastidious moments are noticed on the basis of evidence in his novels, by Gonzalo Sobejano, "El mal poeta de comedias en la narrativa del siglo XVII," *Hispanic Review*, 41 (1973), 313–30, especially 327–28.

7. This is the reasoned view of Juan Antonio Maravall in his *Teatro y literatura en la sociedad barroca*. (Madrid: Hora H. Seminarios y ediciones, 1972), 11–12 and 21–22.

Chapter Two

1. All of the more original poetry of Castillo is informed by this spirit of fun, as the coteries conceived fun, of course. His ability as a writer of verse has possibly been underrated because of centuries of preference for the serious at all costs. Castillo produced many predictably ludicrous pieces on the standard laughing-stocks: incompetent doctors, the defective use of Spanish by both Biscayans and poets of the aureate school *(cultos)*, cosmetics and those physical eyesores beyond the reach of cosmetics. He is naturally attracted to irreverent burlesque of the great stories of antiquity, so that we have, for example, "The Fable of Actaeon and Diana," "Polyphemus," "The Rape of Lucretia," "The Abduction of Europa," "The Fable of Mars and Venus" and "The Fable of Pan and Syrinx," in all of which the mythological figures sink to the status of clowns while the poetic diction remains at Castillo's usual level of talented raillery.

A special place in the works of Castillo is claimed by his piece in verse and prose "The Wedding of the Manzanares" ("Las bodas de Manzanares"), entitled, as it stands in his *Jornadas alegres* (1625), a "fable" but more accurately to be classified as a comical pageant based on personification allegory. The narrative is there to lend support to three longer poems, two in ballad meter and one in *silva*, or free alternation of eleven-syllable and seven-syllable lines. We are to imagine that the ancient Guadarrama has acquired a sprightly and crystalline grandson, the infant Manzanares, the stream which will later flow through the city of Madrid. By its headwaters appear gypsies who foretell its great future and peasants who, like Lilliputians a century later, mistake a saddle and saddlebag floating on the streamlet for an enormous whale. The point of the mention of a whale is to emphasize the ludicrous size of the Manzanares, whose name is a byword for exiguous rivers:

Manzanares, vejete de entremeses,
con justillo, escarcela y capa rota,
no con igual salud todos
los meses,

porque en los más padece mal
de gota,
vuelto de arroyo en charco o
lagunajo,
puede ser entre ríos
espantajo. . . .

Manzanares, old man of an
interlude, with warm undershirt,
pouch and ragged cloak, not equally
healthy every month of the year,
since in most of them he suffers
from gout (also "scarcity of
water-drops"), transformed from
stream into puddle or stagnant pool
he may be called the scarecrow of
rivers. . . .

With the booklet's arrival in Madrid, to the acclamation of the sonnets of Castillo's Academia Mantuana, "His Profundity," the god Neptune confers the title of river on him, so he immediately seeks a wife in, alas, "unequal madrid-mony" *(desigual madridaje)*. A chorus of third-rate rivers, the To-rote, the Zapardiel and other squalid streams provide epithalamia, but the Manzanares is finally not happy. The fanciful piece ends with his writing his complaints, with ink from a swimming-hole where black men have bathed, on a sheet left behind by a riverside washerwoman.

2. An early example of this parade type of interlude, for instance, is the anonymous French *The Poor Devils (Les pauvres diables)* of 1594. We must not forget, either, the "bridal" episode of Francisco López de Úbeda's *The Female Rogue Justina (La pícara Justina*, 1605) in which a series of prospective bridegrooms is paraded for Justina's appraisal. See Francisco J. Sánchez-Díez, *La novela picaresca de protagonista femenino en España durante el siglo XVII*. Unpublished Ph.D. Dissertation, University of North Carolina, Chapel Hill, 1972, p. 50.

3. Gareth Davies. *A Poet at Court: Antonio Hurtado de Mendoza* (Oxford: Dolphin, 1971), 207–21. On the possible influence of Neapolitan literary societies and the physiognomic theories of Giambattista Della Porta (1535–1615) on the Italian farce and the Spanish *entremés* before Mendoza, see Alan Soons, "Los entremeses de Quevedo. Ingeniosidad lingüística y fuerza cómica," *Filologia e letteratura*, 16 (1970), 424–39.

4. The dependency of Castillo is pointed out by Sánchez-Díez, p. 226.

5. Yvonne David-Peyre. *Le Personnage du médecin et la relation médecin-malade dans la littérature ibérique du seizième et du dix-septième siécle* (Paris: Ediciones Hispano-Americanas, 1971), devotes pages 43–47 to *La prueba de los doctores*. She comments on Castillo's mastery of his art and its implications: "The evocation of the scene by expression alone, by mobility of phraseology and by verbal magic, builds up in visual intensity what it inhibits in informative objectivity. It awakens in the hearer a critical attitude towards language." (p. 47). Maxime Chevalier, *Cuentecillos tradicionales en la España del Siglo de Oro* (Madrid: Gredos, 1975), p. 37, shows how this *entremés* derives from Melchor de Santa Cruz's book of anecdotes *Floresta española* (1574).

6. A lucid discussion in the eighteenth century, but of validity in every age, about the strengths and the irrationalities of ridicule, is recounted by Thomas B. Gilmore in *The Eighteenth-Century Controversy over Ridicule as a Test of Truth* (Atlanta: Georgia State University, 1970) especially pp. 26–35. It is quite pertinent to a consideration of Castillo. Ridicule is, it seems, adequate to holding sham and fraud up to contempt and derision, but it ought at some point to yield to rational discourse. This latter alone can lead to creative criticism. Gilmore points out how eighteenth century writers realized that ridicule appears to—and confirms men in—nothing more admirable than preconceived opinions, temperamental predilections, acquired tastes, fashions and local customs. These ephemeral things are exactly what Castillo's "moralizing" is built upon.

Chapter Three

1. Rinaldo Froldi in his *Lope de Vega y la formación de la comedia*, Spanish translation (Madrid: Castalia, 1968) gives the best account of this development.

2. The most comprehensive surveys of the Spanish seventeenth century *comedia* are those of Margaret Wilson. *Spanish Drama of the Golden Age* (Oxford: Pergamon, 1969) and of Duncan Moir in Edward M. Wilson and D. Moir. *A Literary History of Spain. The Golden Age Drama* (London: Benn, 1971).

3. There had been virtually no attention paid to the vigorous Spanish tradition of the nonserious play, either because of the survival of a nineteenth century prejudice or because of the prestige of "Existentialism," until the appearance of the study by Cyril A. Jones: "Some Ways of Looking at Spanish Golden Age Comedy," *Homenaje a William L. Fichter* (Madrid: Castalia, 1971), 329–39. He comments on the essential "liveliness and swift alternation of moods" (333) and cites Martinenche's tribute of 1900 paid to the Spanish comedy for its wholesome effect on the future development of the French comedy (332). Another recent study of the comic in drama of Castillo's age is Amelia Tejada, *Untersuchungen zum Humor in den Comedias Calderóns, unter Ausschluss der "Gracioso"-Gestalten* (Berlin: de Gruyter, 1974).

4. Jones (see note 3), p. 338, cites Northrop Frye's remark that "normal comedy" shows how society in the person of an old man or an outmoded "humor" gives way to a young man's desires.

5. Two excellent discussions of the *gracioso*, as he appears in the plays of Castillo's contemporary Juan Ruiz de Alarcón are J. H. Silverman, "El gracioso de Ruiz de Alarcón," 187–95 and Joaquín Casalduero, "El gracioso de *El Anticristo*," 199–211, both essays now collected in *Critical Essays on the Life and Works of Juan Ruiz de Alarcón*, edited by James A. Parr (Madrid: Dos Continentes, 1972).

6. Jones (p. 336) emphasizes the comparative freedom of the *gracioso* as a character: "The *gracioso* not only tells us what honor or duty or free will means by showing us the negative side . . . . he also tells us what those things mean by showing us what they mean to him, the *gracioso* . . ."

7. See Edwin B. Place, "Notes on the Grotesque: the *Comedia de figurón* at Home and Abroad," "*P M L A*, 54 (1939), 412–21, especially p. 415. Also Jean-Raymond Lanot and Marc Vitse, "Éléments pour une théorie du *figurón*", *Caravelle. Cahiers du monde hispanique et luso-brésilien*, No. 27 (1976), 189–212, especially, for *The Marquis from the Toledo Suburbs*, pp. 200–1.

8. Margaret Wilson, p. 189.

9. Juan Antonio Maravall, p. 135. There is certainly some heavy handed generalization in this work, but Maravall's conclusions do seem to be spe-

cially applicable to secondary dramatists such as Castillo. They are more immediate "mirrors of their age".

10. Herman Meyer in *Der Sonderling in der deutschen Dichtung* (Munich: Hanser, 1963) establishes this definition of the eccentric as a literary figure (pp. 18–21), and proposes that a study of such types will provide a key to an author's conception of humanity and its variety in his epoch.

11. "Gastón" deriving from *"gastar humor"*: "brimming over with wit."

12. The text sometimes calls him Perafán de Ribera, by a printer's oversight no doubt. Afán de Ribera is the name of a notable Seville family, whom Castillo at one time perhaps wished to commemorate, as he did the Marradas of Valencia.

13. Within the ambit of the *comedia*, though premonitory of a tragedy as it happens, we have the scene of the Duke's return from campaigning in Lope de Vega's *Punishment without Revenge* (*El castigo sin venganza*, 1634). Once again the military interlude has clarified the intentions of the lover, in this case of the husband.

14. For an analysis of this play see Alan Soons, "Calderón Dramatizes an Emblem. *No hay cosa como callar*," *Arcadia*, 6 (1971), 72–74.

15. Along with a new ornateness and complexity in plots, and a breaking free from intelligible characterization went an increasing reliance by some playwrights on these mechanical wonders. The notable Italian stage engineer Cosimo Lotti assisted in many spectacles for King Philip IV between 1626 and 1643, though there is no record of his having participated in the production of any of Castillo's pieces (Margaret Wilson, p. 178).

16. This accident is attributed to the fact that the coachman was a Frenchman. This could be an early instance of the perennial whimsy exploited by writers of farces about the French being reckless drivers. Or again it could reflect the anti-French sentiments in Spain at that moment. By 1634 everyone could see that France was adopting a hostile posture towards the Imperial and Spanish side in the Thirty Years' War.

17. This magical alternation between "real" and "spectral" characters appears to derive from Juan Timoneda's *Book of Tales* (*El patrañuelo*, 1567), Tale 13, pp. 153–58 in the edition of Rafael Ferreres, (Madrid: Castalia, 1971), though it is, of course, a topic of romance.

18. The approved adoption of the pose of "secretary" by a nobleman when he "stoops to conquer" is elucidated by Jack W. Sage, "The Context of Comedy. Lope de Vega's *El perro del hortelano* and Related Plays," *Studies in Spanish Literature of the Golden Age, Presented to Edward M. Wilson*, (London: Támesis, 1973), especially pages 262 and 264.

19. For an account of these suburban estates, and of the several etymologies proposed for the name "Cigarrales," see André Nougué *L'Oeuvre en Prose de Tirso de Molina. "Los Cigarrales de Toledo" et "Deleitar Aprovechando"* (Toulouse: Librairie des Facultés, 1962), 144–53, and

also the review of Nougué's work by Gerald E. Wade in *Hispanic Review*, 33 (1965), 246–72, especially pp. 247–50. I have chosen to translate *Cigarrales* as "the Toledo suburbs," partly because of the attitudinizing of the Marquis, and partly because Juan de Mariana, who knew them well, calls them *suburbana praedia* ("suburban estates") in his *De morte et immortalitate* (Cologne: Hieratus, 1609), p. 356.

20. Although Marino is not presented as one of the crass and clownish *graciosos*, his name allows for his appearance wearing seagoing pantaloons, highly amusing for landlubbers. Perhaps this would be expected from an author publishing his book in a seaport, in this case Barcelona.

21. It happens that the Battle of Nördlingen was also celebrated in literature by Gabriel Bocángel Unzueta in his *Infante Ferdinand* (*El Fernando*, 1635), a panegyric with a certain poetic power. It will be found in the reprint of his *Obras*, vol. 1, edited by Rafael Benítez Claros, (Madrid: 1946), 247–57. The matter of Nördlingen occupies pages 254–55. Bocángel makes a similar remark: "*Bien que el gran Duque de Lorena hería / tanto, que España le adoptó aquel día*" ("Although the great Duke of Lorraine dealt / such blows, that Spain adopted him that very day").

22. Since "Zamarra mala" is synonymous with "ruin capa," this name may refer back to the proverb *Bajo ruin capa yace buen bebedor* (Under a miserable cloak may be found a good drinker).

23. The details of the historical battle are conveniently set out in C. B. Malleson, *The Battle-Fields of Germany* (Reprinted Westport, Connecticut: Greenwood Press, 1971), pp. 117–24.

24. Bocángel seizes on the incident for a pretty simile: *Cual huye al bosque incauto conejuelo / a sombra del cañón, del miedo alado, / el escuadrón sueco elige un suelo / de engaños y de robres trincherado, / y opuesto en su labor al propio intento, / su laberinto obró su monumento.* (Just as the surprised rabbit runs into the copse, flying with fear to the shadows of its burrow, so the Swedish squadron selects a terrain trenched with mines and oaken logs. Yet they worked in the event against their own intentions and their labyrinth became their grave-monument).

25. Bocángel presents a rather similar Weimar: *Oyense de Vehimar altas blasfemias, / que el cielo manchan de veneno y muerte, . . .* (Great blasphemies are heard from Weimar, which stain the heavens with poison and death).

26. Castillo lacks the epic voice to praise the deeds of the Spanish forces, while Bocángel makes them very memorable: *Los olimpos de acero, o españoles, / hacen, y los demás sufren, la guerra, . . .* (Those Olympians of steel, I mean the Spaniards, make war, while the others merely suffer it).

27. By Franco Bacchelli. "Castillo Solórzano, *El fuego dado del cielo.* Edizione, introduzione e note," *Miscellanea di studi ispanici. I-Letteratura classica* (Pisa: Università di Pisa, 1974), pp. 181–268. Bacchelli (p. 192) comments on several characteristics which link this work with Castillo's

usual secular pieces: his inability to represent a Cyrus inimical to Judaism; the passionless love-story, here quite adventitious in the text; on the other hand, his mastery of dialogue and his unfailing cheerfulness.

Chapter Four

1. By Gonzalo Sobejano in his review of Stuart Miller, *The Picaresque Novel* in *Hispanic Review*, 40 (1972), 323. A very fine survey of the limits of the picaresque genre is to be found in the first chapter of the already cited unpublished dissertation of Francisco Javier Sánchez-Díez.

2. Sánchez-Díez points out that already Salas Barbadillo had exploited the theme: he has a novella called "El coche mendigón, envergonzante y endemoniado" ("The Shameful, Wheedling and Devilish Coach") dated 1620 and in his interlude "Las aventureras en la Corte" ("Adventuresses in Madrid") of 1622 he uses the term "harpies," but puts his gold-diggers to work in mantles "of respectability" rather than in coaches (Sánchez-Díez, p. 203).

3. Dunn, p. 14, points out the connection between this fictional scaffolding and Boccaccio's device of appointing a "queen for the day" on each of the ten days of his *Decameron*.

4. The tension between the good example of these kind, but despised, protectresses and her bad inclinations forms the psychological ground of the story. Her inclinations prevail so that she becomes in her turn a "Proteus," never achieving repose. (Sánchez-Díez, p. 217).

5. Teresa is herself astonished at the thought that any woman could entertain affection for a eunuch, and makes a "masculine" remark on the occasion. Castillo, then, may have allowed his female character to slip inadvertently into the way of thinking of a male counterpart. See Thomas Hanrahan. *La mujer en la novela picaresca española* (Madrid: Porrúa, 1967), p. 227.

6. Sánchez-Díaz, p. 216.

7. This restlessness is, of course, extremely useful to Castillo in his concern to weld together a sequence of disparate episodes. See Cunningham, p. 15. Frequently quoted, and deservedly, is Castillo's evocation of Madrid at the beginning of *The Harpies*. It conveys just this febrile movement and the ambitions which this can inspire:

. . . . en comparación con Madrid, corte del español monarca, cada una de estas ciudades [*scil*. Granada and Córdoba] es una aldea. ¿Que digo aldea? ¡Un solitario cortijo!

Es Madrid un maremágnum donde todo bajel navega, desde el

In comparison with Madrid, the capital of the Spanish monarch, any one of these cities is a village. Did I say village? An out-of-the-way hamlet!

Madrid is a wide ocean where every kind of craft is sailing, from the most powerful galleon down to the most humble and insignificant

más poderoso galéon hasta el más
humilde y
pequeño esquife; . . . . Es
el refugio de todo
peregrino viviente,
el amparo de todos
los que la buscan; su
grandeza anima a vivir
en ella; su trato
hechiza y su confusión
alegra. ¿Qué humilde
sujeto no engrandece
y muda de condición
para aspirar a mayor
parte? ¿Qué linaje
oscuro y bajo no se
bautizó con nuevo
apellido para pasar
plaza de noble?
Finalmente . . . es el
lugar de los milagros
y el centro de las
transformaciones.

skiff; . . . It is the refuge of every
living wanderer [or "every strange
individual"], the shelter of all who
seek her; her grandeur incites one
to live there; familiarity with her
fascinates and her tumult
exhilarates. What humble person
does not grow in stature and change
social class in order to aspire to
greater things? What obscure
pedigree has not christened itself
with a new surname in order to pass
itself off as noble? In a word . . . it
is the theater of miracles and the
arena of transformations.

8. Sánchez-Díez, p. 218.

9. The defects of character of her natural parents were by no means frightful, it will be remembered. Stigma is then something derived from a more general heredity. (Sánchez-Díez, p. 215).

10. Thomas Hanrahan, S. J. *La mujer en la novela picaresca española* (Madrid: Porrúa, 1967), p. 227.

11. She calls her kindly guardians avaricious, though we see no evidence of this in the episodes she relates of them. (Cunningham, p. 13).

12. Cunningham, pp. 116–17.

13. Cunningham, p. 9.

14. Sánchez-Díez, p. 224.

15. Cunningham, p. 23, observes her faculty for remembering without effort fifty lines of verse composed by Sarabia.

16. Leonardo is flatly stated to have been incapable of overhearing Teresa's conversation. Also, her memories of the life of her mother in the remote past strain our credulity a little (Cunningham, pp. 21–22). The same commentator establishes the rule that such characters must be persevering (or the episodes will peter out); must fail (or the didactic pretension is ruined); and must never profit from experience (or he or she will become self-aware and disillusioned), p. 37. In the light of this it follows that the warning contained in the story is presumably for possible victims of such cheats, not for possible imitators. (Sánchez-Díez, p. 212).

17. The literary and sub-literary reports of the career and amorous ad-

ventures of the celebrated Nun-Ensign *(monja alférez)*, sometimes given the name Catalina de Erauso, are described in some detail by Helen P. Houck, *"La monja alférez.* Woman of Mystery," *Hispania,* 22 (1939), 215–16. This female soldier certainly existed, but the nun with the name Catalina de Erauso had a different career altogether. It is surmised that the *alférez* usurped a comrade's sister's name.

18. Cunningham, p. 94, cites this as a good example of Castillo's own dread of the atypical.

19. Sánchez-Díez, p. 79, joins others in speculating that Castillo hit upon this idea of linking stories in emulation of the "cycles" of Spanish novels of chivalry.

20. Cunningham, pp. 75–81, maintains that these particular interpolated stories reveal baser passions in their courtly characters than those set in the earlier books, and most of those in independent collections.

21. Rufina is usually diffident about men, but Jaime overwhelms her at their meeting. Is this the hidden power of ambition which is in him?

22. These interpolations indeed divide the story into three major sections, each dominated by a spectacular swindle: of Marquina, of Octavio Filuchi, and of Crispín.

23. Cunningham, p. 97, relates this perception to the Aristotelian rules of decorum; the authority of the three styles, high, low and mixed, is what ultimately frustrates Trapaza's climb into the higher strata of society!

24. Trapaza's intrepidity is the cause of his death. Yet when he was confronted by the minor character Don Enrique, a man "of quality," he had taken to his heels. (Cunningham, p. 40).

25. Sánchez-Díez, p. 129.

26. Cunningham, p. 61, observes the pronounced literary proclivities of Estefanía and Rufina, and speculates on the appeal Castillo might have been intending to make to his female readers.

27. Sánchez-Díez, p. 132, is of the opinion that López de Úbeda's female prankster, the *Pícara Justina,* is really a kind of emanation from the male *pícaro,* specifically from Aleman's Guzmán de Alfarache. Úbeda merely changes the sex of the main character, and even allows *her* to proffer his own misogynistic platitudes. Justina's femininity is one more stigma comparable to that of being a "new Christian."

28. Sánchez-Díez, p. 187.

29. Sánchez-Díez, p. 121.

30. Both women, however, deceive their older husbands without compunction as though it were their right. Cunningham, (p. 46), see Estefanía as a notably stable personality, and perhaps less reprehensible than the three ladies of quality, of whom Trapaza sees the grasping and worldly side: Antonia, Brianda and Serafina.

31. Hanrahan, p. 245.

32. If minor characters happen to be of the gentry, and therefore "deco-

rous," they may lose sums of money to a charming *buscona* or a personable cheat. Castillo presents this loss as worth the adventure. (Cunningham, 49).

33. Castillo tends to show the side of religion which is closest to materialism: Crispín, for example, is an exploiter of others' generosity *(The She-Stoat)*, and Lorenzo an exploiter of the Church's economic power *(Trapaza).* Justice is on the whole mocked in Castillo's works: stolen property is seldom recovered, lawsuits are interminable and fatuous, inheritances vanish, while *pícaros* take advantage of the often unjust blame automatically cast on passing soldiers for offences. (Cunningham, 111; 115–17).

34. Castillo has, however, a double standard of moral judgment when it comes to the rich: if they are *indianos* (those who have enriched themselves in America) or inheritors (that is, Spanish) they are approved of; if they are foreigners, they are unprincipled skinflints. (Cunningham, 125).

35. The *pícaro's* plans are ultimately undone by "the cosmos" (and of course, the omnipotent author Castillo). These moral stories are, then, delineations of the action of causality and scarcely moral at all in that they show the exceptional, not the everyday which the reader has to make moral choices in.

Chapter Five

1. This useful division is that of Sarah Nemtzow, *Castillo Solórzano, An Analysis of his Novelistic Production,* Unpublished Ph.D. dissertation, University of California at Los Angeles, 1952.

2. Florence L. Yudin, "Theory and Practice of the *Novela comediesca," Romanische Forschungen,* 81 (1969), 585–94.

3. Willard F. King, *Prosa novelística y academias literarias en el siglo XVII,* Madrid, (1963), p. 214.

4. Florence L. Yudin, "The *Novela corta* as Comedia. Lope's *Las fortunas de Diana," Bulletin of Hispanic Studies,* 45 (1968), 181–88, especially pp. 183–84.

5. Yudin, "Theory and Practice of the *Novela comediesca,"* p. 585.

6. Francisco Yndurain, *Lope de Vega como novelador* (Santander: Isla de los ratones, 1962), pp. 76–77. The practice of Lope de Vega as writer of novellas and that of Castillo are entirely comparable.

7. Yudin, "The *Novela corta* as *Comedia,"* pp. 182–83.

8. A good recent treatment of this recourse on the part of tellers of tales is that of Morton W. Bloomfield, "Authenticating Realism and the Realism of Chaucer," *Essays and Explorations* (Cambridge, Massachusetts: Harvard University Press, 1970), especially pages 181 and 190.

9. King, pp. 127–28.

10. King, p. 214.

11. Dunn, *Castillo Solórzano,* p. 58.

12. Yndurain, p. 46.

13. Ynduráin, p. 27.

14. Dunn, p. 41.

15. The term is commented on by Ynduráin, p. 64.

16. There is a recent and painstaking examination of the question of the sincerity of Spanish seventeenth century authors of novellas with explicit moral intention in Joseph B. Spieker, "La novela ejemplar. 'Delectare— prodesse,' " *Iberoromania*, Neue Folge, No. 2 (1975), 33–68.

Chapter Six

1. An abridged translation of the narrative as it is spoken by the Count of the Kitchen Garden himself may be of value to comparative folklorists for this reason:

"The Infanta Teodomira fell in love with Recaredo the Gallant, one of the great nobles of Galicia. She was related to him, but not closely, and he was able to gain entry into the Infanta's room and to deserve her embrace. From that amorous union I was born.

On giving birth to me my mother went out and handed me over to one of her brothers who threw me into the river Sil through a door which looked out on to it, in a wicker basket. It was floating along when the water divided and I was submerged and taken up into the arms of the genius of the Sil who was surrounded by his beautiful nymphs. I was taken to his crystalline apartments, where I was brought up by the nymphs and instructed by the ancient genius of the river.

Among that virginal choir of nymphs was one whom the ancient Sil held in more esteem than the others. She was called Anacarsia, a prodigy in everything. I felt a passion for this beauty, and one day while the nymphs were away at a performance of music and verse with which they entertained Father Sil, she feigned an illness. I was made aware of this ruse and went to her room, where I found her in her own soft bed. Anacarsia felt love for me, showed me favor and a hope of further delights, had not the steps of the wavy Sil not cut it all short. He was able to overhear all our talk of love, became angry with me and would not allow my audacity to go further. He surrounded the apartment of Anacarsia with clear waves, covered the door where she lived, pulled me out from there violently and from thence to the river bank. I heard a voice saying: "Gundemaro, you are the descendant of kings. You were born a pagan, but you will choose the religion which best suits you, that which this kingdom holds. Your expulsion from my abode has been a just one, because it was unreasonable to allow an illicit love with one who has offered her purity to me, and whom I protect."

He said this and with one swirl he stirred up the water, which immediately afterwards became quiet again as though nothing had happened. I found myself in a kitchen garden, in a bed sown with parsley. From that place I take my name, and after baptism I called myself Pero Gil de Galicia, taking my surname from the kingdom which was my parents', who had died four hundred years before.

So it is that I am the Count of the Kitchen Garden, a title which I have conferred on myself, for a man as illustrious as I cannot pass his life as an ordinary gentleman."

Luciano García Lorenzo, *El tema del conde Alarcos. Del Romancero a Jacinto Grau*, (Madrid 1972) examines Castillo's debt to the narrative material of the ballad "Conde Alarcos" (pp. 89–92). This is a short novella set in ancient Rome and interpolated in *El bachiller Trapaza*.

2. For a discussion of this theory of *entremés* origins and also of the special features of Quevedo's productions, see Alan Soons, "Los entremeses de Quevedo. Ingeniosidad lingüística y fuerza cómica," *Filología e letteratura*, 16 (1970), 424–39.

3. A good introduction to this area of literature and sub-literature in English, and referring to English literature in particular, is that of Erland Munch-Petersen,, "Trivial Literature and Mass-Reading," *Orbis litterarum*, 27 (1972), 157–78.

4. These characteristics are enumerated especially well by Wolfgang Binder in his "Dichtung und Trivialliteratur," collected into his volume *Literatur als Denkschule* (Zürich and Munich: Artemis, 1972), pp. 17–26, and also by Thomas Koebner in his "Zum Wertungsproblem in der Trivialromanforschung," *Vergleichen und verändern. Festschrift für H. Motekat* (Munich: Heuber, 1970), pp. 74–105. Koebner makes a list of certain constants: (1) Unawareness of problems, in the story or in society; no empiricism; (2) Simplicity of interpretation; (3) Motivation never complex, the structure of the novelist's consciousness being always commensurable with the reader's; (4) A tendency to resort to worked-out formal devices; (5) Irrational elements unresolved in the tendency the story has to linearity; (6) Contemporary reality and everyday places avoided; the mythical in any threatening aspect emptied out (p. 100).

5. Binder, p. 21.

6. Binder, p. 24.

7. Another useful essay among the myriad published in Germany on the subject of trivial (i.e., "purveyed") literature is that of Hans Friedrich Foltin, "Zur Erforschung der Unterhaltungs—und Trivialliteratur, insbesondere im Bereich des Romans" in *Studien zur Trivialliteratur*, edited by H. O. Burger, (Frankfurt: Klostermann, 1968) pp. 242–70. These contrasts with "higher" fiction are examined on p. 265.

8. Nemtzow, *Castillo Solórzano*, pp. 319–20.

9. Nemtzow, p. 274.

10. Dunn, *Castillo Solórzano*, p. 91.

11. Cf., on this point, Hermann Bausinger, "Schwierigkeiten bei der Untersuchung von Trivialliteratur," *Wirkendes Wort*, 13 (1963), 214–5.

12. Dunn, p. 80.

13. Dunn, p. 75.

14. Juan Antonio Maravall propounds this thesis in his *Teatro y literatura en la sociedad barroca* (Madrid: Hora H. Seminarios y Ediciones, 1972), p. 32.

15. Dunn, p. 91.

16. A good discussion of this type of literature in Spanish is that of José María Díez Borque, *Literatura y cultura de masas* (Barcelona: Al-Borak,

1972). While mainly studying the *novelas rosa* and Westerns of our own times he examines some precursors of these in past ages, p. 65.

17. Maravall, p. 52.

18. See René Godenne, *Histoire de la Nouvelle française aux 17e et 18e siècles* (Geneva: Droz, 1970), p. 29.

19. Godenne, pp. 37 and 49–50.

20. Frederick A. De Armas. *Paul Scarron* (New York: Twayne, 1972) describes (pp. 76–81 and 124–128) the extent of Scarron's borrowings from Castillo. There is an illuminating account of the intelligent use Scarron made of these stories in his own novel of theatrical life, in the same author's *The Four Interpolated Stories in the* Roman comique. *Their Sources and Unifying Function* (Chapel Hill, University of N. Carolina Press, 1971), where Castillo is considered (pp. 76–81).

21. Another minor borrowing by a French author is studied by Henry Carrington Lancaster in "Castillo Solórzano's 'El celoso hasta la muerte' and Montfleury's *École des Jaloux*," *Modern Language Notes*, 54 (1939), 436–7. D. L. Drysdall's "Molière and Spain. A Bibliographical Survey," *A U M L A*, 39 (1973), 94–112, could have shown the French dramatist's indebtedness to much better advantage.

22. Godenne, p. 243.

23. The relative readiness of French and English readers of fiction for translations of Castillo is illustrated by Joseph E. Tucker, "Castillo's *Garduña de Sevilla* in English Translation," *Papers of the Bibliographical Society of America*, 46 (1952), 154–8.

24. John J. Richetti, *Popular Fiction Before Richardson. Narrative Patterns 1700–1739* (Oxford: Clarendon Press, 1969), gives the best account of the type of story which was invented as a consequence of the translations of Castillo, among others, in his chapters "Rogues and Whores. Heroes and Anti-Heroes," pp. 23–59 and "Mrs. Hayward and the Novella. The Erotic and the Pathetic," pp. 168–210.

25. Cunningham, *Castillo Solórzano*, p. 137, compares Defoe's treatment of Moll Flanders with Castillo's of his *busconas* in that in both cases we learn more about how to practise confidence-tricks than about the moral sanction against them. The contrast may be established, however, between the two types of heroine in that Moll has a "vegetable tropism," leading her ever towards inertia and security (Cf. the notorious "repose" finally wished for by the Princess of Clèves in Madame de Lafayette's novel), while Castillo's women never betray diminished energy and restlessness.

Chapter Seven

1. Paulo Charquías (Pau Jarquies) of Barcelona, pioneer of refrigeration in Spain, who made use of snow deposits in warm weather.

2. Here and elsewhere, Castillo uses the more or less jocular figure of the Jews' patience in waiting for the Messiah.

3. The lines in italics are from ancient ballads.

4. Conde Claros, Durandarte, the Aliatares, Zaide and Zaida, *et al.* are characters well-known in the ballads.

5. The reference is to the statue dreamed of by the King of Babylon, with "unworthy" feet. *Daniel,* II, 32–34.

6. A burlesque ballad-hero, whose posterior tends to become suddenly exposed. Cf. R. Menéndez Pidal, in *Bulletin hispanique,* 50 (1948), 305–12.

7. The river, subsiding into stagnant pools resembles a fragmented glass.

8. Castillo plays here with notions of poetic "feet" and "glosses," as in his "Mantuan" academy.

9. Zoilus, the legendary sophist who typifies the critic whom it is impossible to satisfy: Momus, the ancients' god of mockery.

10. Castillo plays, of course, on *"flaco"* and *"osar."*

11. Attis was transformed into the pine tree (Ovid. *Metamorphoses,* X, 105).

12. Apparently Castillo is invoking *"cuernos"* and *"topo"* (blind, but one who may find it convenient to be sightless).

13. The Latin tag *Necessitas caret lege* (as in XIV) is at the root of this otherwise meaningless expression.

14. The "Gold Coast" of West Africa.

15. A well-known play on the word *"botín."* Alexander the Great became a byword in antiquity for his generosity.

16. Castillo is referring to alternative meanings of *"blanca"* (a small coin) and *"tecla"* (key or chord of a musical instrument).

Selected Bibliography

In the absence of any definitive collection or edition of the complete works of Castillo Sorzano, information is given as to the contents of the volumes listed below.

PRIMARY SOURCES

Donayres del Parnaso. Primera parte. Madrid: Flamenco, 1624. (*Segunda parte.* Madrid: Flamenco, 1625) Never reprinted. Two ballads are reprinted in Maxime Chevalier. *Cuentecillos tradicionales en la España del Siglo de Oro.* Madrid: Gredos ("Biblioteca Románica Hispánica. IV—Textos," 9). These are: "Al suceso de un novio que trocó la noche de su boda una bebida con la purga de un enfermo" ("On the Occasion of a Bridegroom's Mistaking, on his Wedding Night, and Invalid's Purge for his Own Drink") and its counterpart "Al suceso del enfermo, con la confección que estaba para el novio" ("On the Occasion of the Invalid's Swallowing the Brew Intended for the Bridegroom"), pages 146–50.

Tardes entretenidas. Madrid: Martín, 1625. Reprinted Madrid: Maestre, 1908 ("Colección selecta de antiguas novelas españolas," 9). Contains the novellas "El amor en la venganza," "La fantasma de Valencia," "El Proteo de Madrid," "El socorro en el peligro," "El culto graduado" and "Engañar con la verdad."

Jornadas alegres. Madrid: González, 1626. Reprinted Madrid: Maestre, 1909 ("Colección selecta de antiguas novelas españolas," 11). Contains the novellas "No hay mal que no venga por bien," "La obligación cumplida," "La cruel aragonesa," "La libertad merecida" and "El obstinado arrepentido," besides the allegorical fable in prose and verse "Fábula de las bodas de Manzanares."

Tiempo de regocijo y Carnestolendas de Madrid. Madrid: Sánchez, 1627. Reprinted Madrid: Maestre, 1907, ("Colección selecta de antiguas novelas españolas," 7). Contains the novellas "El duque de Milán," "La quinta de Diana" and "El ayo de su hijo," besides the interlude "El

casamentero." "La quinta de Diana," retitled "La quinta de Laura" in
reprinted *Novelas amorosas de los mejores ingenios de España.*
Zaragoza: Verges, 1648, and Alfay, 1649, and Barcelona: Vassiana 1650,
and Madrid: Sancha, 1777. ("Colección de obras sueltas de Lope de
Vega, 8). "El casamentero" reprinted Madrid: Bailly-Bailliere, 1911
("Nueva biblioteca de autores españoles," 17), 303–09.

Escarmientos de amor moralizados. Sevilla: Sande, 1628. Never reprinted.

Lisardo enamorado. Valencia: Garriz, 1629. Reprinted Madrid: Ultra, 1947
("Biblioteca selecta de clásicos españoles," 3).

Huerta de Valencia. Prosas y versos en las academias della. Valencia:
Sorolla, 1629. Reprinted Madrid: Aldus, 1944 ("Sociedad de Bibliófilos
Españoles. Segunda época," 15). Contains the novellas "El amor por la
piedad," "El defensor contra sí," "El soberbio castigado" and "La
duquesa de Mantua," besides the play "El agravio satisfecho." The four
novellas reprinted, Madrid: Imprenta Real, 1789 ("Colección de
novelas escogidas," 7) and "El agravio satisfecho" reprinted, Barcelona:
Casa Provincial de Caridad, 1943.

Las harpías en Madrid, y coche de las estafas. Barcelona: Cormellas, 1631.
Reprinted Barcelona: Cormellas, 1633 and Madrid: Maestre, 1907
("Colección selecta de antiguas novelas españolas," 7). Contains an
untitled novella stated to be adapted from the Italian of Sansovino, and
the interlude "El comisario de figuras." This last reprinted Madrid:
Bailly-Bailliere, 1911 ("Nueva biblioteca de autores españoles," 17)
309–12. There is a facsimile reprint, by G. Rozzano, Milan: La Goliar-
dica, 1966.

*Noches de placer, en que contiene doce novelas, dirigidas a diversos títulos y
caballeros de Valencia.* Barcelona: Cormellas, 1631. Reprinted Madrid: Ibérica, 1906 ("Colección selecta de antiguas novelas españolas," 5)
and Barcelona: Maucci, 1914 and 1922 ("Biblioteca de clásicos selec-
tos"). Contains the novellas "Las dos dichas sin pensar," "La cautela sin
efecto," "La ingratitud y el castigo," "El inobediente," "Atrevimiento y
ventura," "El hacer bien no se pierde," "El pronóstico cumplido," "La
fuerza castigada," "El celoso hasta la muerte," "El ingrato Federico,"
"El honor recuperado" and "El permio de la virtud." "Las dos dichas
sin pensar," "El pronóstico cumplido" and "El celoso hasta la muerte"
reprinted in *Novelas amorosas de los mejores ingenios de España.*
Zaragoza: Verges, 1648 and Alfay, 1649, and Barcelona: Vassiana, 1650.
"Las dos venturas *(sic)* sin pensar," "El pronóstico cumplido" and "El
celoso hasta morir *(sic)*" Madrid: Sancha, 1777 ("Colección de obras
sueltas de Lope de Vega," 8).

Favores de las musas hechos a don Francisco de Medrano. Milan: Malatesta,
1631. Never reprinted.

La niña de los embustes Teresa de Manzanares, natural de Madrid. Barcelona: Margarit, 1632. Reprinted Madrid: Rico, 1906 ("Colección

selecta de antiguas novelas españolas," 3), Madrid: Aguilar, 1929 ("Colección de autores regocijados," 4) and 1964 ("Colección Crisol," 21), and New York: Instituto de las Españas, 1936. Also in *La novela picaresca española.* Madrid: Aguilar, 1943 ("Colección Obras Eternas"). Contains the interludes "La prueba de los doctores" and "El barbador," reprinted Madrid: Bailly-Bailliere, 1911 ("Nueva biblioteca de autores españoles," 17), 312–18.

Los amantes andaluces. Historia entretenida. Prosas y versos. Barcelona: Cormellas, 1633. Reprinted Hildesheim: Olms, 1973.

Fiestas del jardín, que contienen tres comedias y cuatro novelas. Valencia: Esparsa, 1634. Reprinted Hildesheim: Olms, 1973. Contains the novellas "La vuelta del ruiseñor," "La injusta ley derogada," "Los hermanos parecidos" and "La crianza bien lograda," besides the plays "Los encantos de Bretaña," "La fantasma de Valencia" and "El marqués del Cigarral." "El marqués del Cigarral" reprinted in *Doce comedias. Segunda parte.* Lisbon: Álvarez, 1647, in *Primavera numerosa de muchas armonías lucientes.* Madrid: 1679, Valladolid: Riego, c. 1730, Burgos (attributed to Agustín Moreto): Imprenta de la Santa Iglesia, c. 1740 and Madrid: Rivadeneyra, 1858 ("Biblioteca de autores españoles," 45).

"Respuesta a este romance" (i.e. "De un amigo a quien convidó el autor, para la Academia, una noche de invierno") in *Segunda parte de las comedias del Maestro Tirso de Molina, recogidas por su sobrino don Francisco Lucas de Ávila.* Madrid: Reino, 1635. Reprinted Madrid: Bailly-Bailliere, 1906 ("Nueva biblioteca de autores españoles," 4), lxxxii (cols. 1–2).

Sagrario de Valencia, en quien se incluyen las vidas de los ilustres santos hijos suyos y del Reino. Valencia: Esparsa, 1635. Never reprinted.

Patrón de Alcira. El glorioso mártir San Bernardo de la Orden del Cister. Zaragoza: Verges, 1636. Never reprinted.

Aventuras del bachiller Trapaza, quintaesencia de embusteros y maestro de embelecadores. Zaragoza: Vergés, 1637. Reprinted Madrid: Alonso y Padilla, 1733, Madrid: Yenes, 1844, Madrid: El Tiempo, 1880, Pozuelo de Alarcón: Minuesa, 1905 ("Biblioteca picaresca," 1), Madrid: Atlas, 1944 ("Colección Cisneros," 78), Madrid: Pérez Capó, 1944, Madrid: Castilla, 1949 ("Biblioteca clásica Castilla") and Madrid: Alonso, 1966. Also in *La novela picaresca española.* Madrid: Aguilar, 1943 ("Colección Obras Eternas"). Contains an untitled novella about two characters Claudio and Porcia, and another one later reprinted with the title "El pretendiente oculto y casamiento efectuado" in *Colección de novelas escogidas.* Madrid: Imprenta Real, 1749, vol. 6. Also includes the interlude "La castañera," reprinted Madrid: Bailly-Bailliere, 1911 ("Nueva biblioteca de autores españoles," 17), 318–21.

Historia de Marco Antonio y Cleopatra, última reina de Egipto. Zaragoza:

Vergés, 1639. Reprinted Madrid: Alonso y Padilla, 1736 and Barcelona: Porter, 1947 (with water-colors by Andrés Lambert).

Epítome de la vida y hechos del ínclito rey don Pedro de Aragón, tercero deste nombre, cognominado el Grande, hijo del esclarecido rey don Jayme el Conquistador. Zaragoza: Dormer, 1639. Never reprinted.

Los alivios de Casandra. Barcelona: Romeu, 1640. Never reprinted. Contains the novellas "La confusión de una noche," "A un engaño otro mayor," "Los efectos que hace amor," "Amor con amor se paga" and "En el delito el remedio," besides the play "El mayorazgo figura." "El mayorazgo figura" reprinted Madrid: Rivadeneyra, 1858 ("Biblioteca de autores españoles," 45) and Barcelona: Manero, 1867 ("Teatro selecto antiguo y moderno," 3).

Sala de recreación. Zaragoza: Lanaja, 1640 and 1649. Never reprinted. Contains the novellas "La dicha merecida," "El disfrazado," "Más puede amor que la sangre," "Escarmiento de atrevidos" and "Las pruebas en la mujer," besides the play "La torre de Florisbella" and a short pageant *(sarao).* "El disfrazado," "Más puede amor que la sangre" and "Escarmiento de atrevidos" reprinted Madrid: Imprenta Real, 1788 ("Colección de novelas escogidas," 3) and "El disfrazado" reprinted Madrid: Rivadeneyra, 1854 ("Biblioteca de autores españoles," 33). The edition of 1640 occurs only in Gallardo's list and may not have existed.

La garduña de Sevilla y anzuelo de las bolsas. Madrid: Reino, 1642. Reprinted Barcelona: Cormellas, 1644, Madrid: Alonso y Padilla, 1733, Madrid: Espasa-Calpe, 1922 ("Clásicos castellanos," 42) and in *La novela picaresca española.* Madrid: Aguilar, 1943 ("Colección Obras eternas"). Includes the novellas "Quien todo lo quiere todo lo pierde," "El conde de las legumbres" and "A lo que obliga el honor." "El conde de las legumbres" reprinted Madrid: Patronato Social, c. 1914 ("Biblioteca de cultura popular," 23).

La quinta de Laura, que contiene seis novelas, adornadas de diferentes versos. Zaragoza: Real Hospital, 1649. Reprinted Madrid: Alonso y Padilla, 1732. Includes the novellas "La ingratitud castigada," "La inclinación española," "El desdén vuelto en favor," "No hay mal que no venga por bien" (i. e. a second novella with that title, this time entirely lacking the letter *i*), "Lances de amor y fortuna" and "El duende de Zaragoza." It is probable that neither frame-story nor novellas are by Castillo in their entirety. "La inclinatión española" reprinted Madrid: Imprenta Real, 1749 ("Colección de novelas escogidas," 3). Madrid: Rivadeneyra, 1854 ("Biblioteca de autores españolas," 33) and Madrid: Patronato Social, c. 1914 ("Biblioteca de cultura popular," 23).

"La victoria de Norlingen y el Infante en Alemania," in *Parte veinte y ocho de comedias nuevas. . . .* Madrid: Fernández de Buendía, 1667. Never reprinted.

I. Translations into English

La Pícara, or the Triumphs of Female Subtilty. Display'd in the Artifices and Impostures of a Beautiful Woman, who Treppan'd the Most Experienc'd Rogues. By John Davies of Cydweli. London: Starkey, 1665 (from *La niña de los embustes*).

The Spanish Decameron. By R(oger) L('Estrange). London: Neale, 1687; London: Harris, 1712; London: Bowyer, 1720. (The three novellas and chapters 4–6 and 6–9 from *La garduña de Sevilla.* L'Estrange changes the names of characters and supplies titles of his own: "The Perfidious Mistress," "The Metamorphos'd Lover," "The Impostour Out-Witted," "The Amorous Miser" and "The Pretended Alchymist." A novella from the French of Marguérite de Navarre is interpolated in "The Pretended Alchymist").

Three Ingenious Spanish Novels. By a Person of Quality (i.e. John Davies of Cydweli). London: Tracy, 1712 [alleged second edition]. From a previous French adaptation of Castillo, yielding the titles: "The Loving Revenge," "The Lucky Escape" and "The Witty Extravagant" from "El amor en la venganza," "El socorro en el peligro" and "El culto graduado," all from *Tardes entretenidas*).

The Life of Donna Rosina. By E(dward) W(aldron). London: Harris, c. 1703. (from *La garduña de Sevilla*).

The Spanish Pole-Cat, or the Adventures of Seniora Rufina. By Roger L'Estrange and John Ozell. London: Curll and Taylor, 1717. (From *La garduña de Sevilla*).

Spanish Amusements, or the Adventures of that Celebrated Courtezan Seniora Rufina. In Six Novels. London: Curll, 1727 and 1741. (Reproduces *The Spanish Pole-Cat*).

The Spanish Rogues, being the History of Donna Rossina. Dublin: M'Donnel, 1792. (Reproduces *The Life of Donna Rosina*).

SECONDARY SOURCES

Books, Monographs, Critical Editions:

COTARELO MORI, EMILIO. "Introducción" to *La niña de los embustes.* Madrid: 1906 ("Colección selecta de antiguas novelas españolas," 3) A full, but by now unreliable treatment of Castillo's life and activities. There is some introductory material in other books of this series: 5 (*Noches de placer*); 7 (*Las harpías en Madrid* and *Tiempo de regocijo*, 1907); 9 (*Tardes entretenidas*, 1908) and 11 (*Jornadas alegres*, 1909).

CUNNINGHAM, MALCOLM A. *Castillo Solórzano. A Reappraisal.* Unpublished dissertation, Tulane University, 1971. Analyses the longer novels of Castillo from the standpoint of recent critical method: authorial presence is traced and Castillo's ability to sustain Teresa's "autobiography" is estimated.

DUNN, PETER N. *Castillo Solórzano and the Decline of the Spanish Novel*. Oxford: Blackwell, 1952. 141 pages. An excellent survey, marred only by certain moralizing conclusions, pertinent perhaps to the time of writing. There is an inclination towards an intolerance of Castillo, resulting in his being measured against "higher literature" and found wanting.

GUTIÉRREZ, FERANANDO. "Prólogo" to *Historia de Marco Antonio y Cleopatra*. Barcelona: Porter, 1947. pp. 5–9. Repeats the remarks of previous literary historians, with more stylishness.

HANRAHAN, THOMAS, S. J. *La mujer en la novela picaresca española*. Madrid: Porrúa, 1967 ("Biblioteca Tenanitla," 10). Studies (II, 226–61) Castillo's characters Teresa and Rufina, and suggests that such women are better described as *busconas* (freelance swindlers) than as *pícaras* (a designation which he thinks ought to imply that the rogue has a master).

KING, WILLARD F. *Prosa novelística y academias literarias en el siglo XVII*. Madrid: 1963 ("Anejos del Boletín de la Real Academia Española," 10). The pioneering study, completely authoritative and often very amusing, of the literary societies which were Castillo's element, and their repercussions on the production of novels.

JULIÁ MARTÍNEZ, EDUARDO. "Observaciones preliminares" to *La Huerta de Valencia*, Madrid: 1944 ("Sociedad de bibliófilos españoles. Segunda época," 15), vii-xl. Some new and more accurate biographical material. This author is fond of unsupported assertions about Castillo's "contributions to realism" and the "continuous development of his art."

———, "Observaciones preliminares" to *Lisardo enamorado*. Madrid: 1947 ("Biblioteca selecta de clásicos españoles. Segunda serie," 3), 7–52. More or less the same content as the previous item, but destined for a public wider than that of the group of bibliophiles.

NEMTZOW, SARAH. *Alonso de Castillo Solórzano. An Analysis of his Novelistic Production*. Unpublished dissertation, University of California at Los Angeles, 1952. A good analysis of all the novellas and novels of swindling, but finally indecisive as to Castillo's stature and good features.

RUIZ MORCUENDE, FEDERICO. "Prólogo" to *La garduña de Sevilla*. Madrid: Espasa-Calpe, 1942 ("Clásicos castellanos," 42), vii-xxxii. Repeats Cotarelo to a great extent, but very insistent on seeing Castillo as a "precursor" of the modern novel.

SÁNCHEZ-DÍEZ, FRANCISCO JAVIER. *La novela picaresca de protagonista femenino en España durante el siglo XVII*. Unpublished dissertation, University of North Carolina, Chapel Hill, 1972. An innovative and patient clarification of the whole subject. The chapter "La picaresca femenina en Castillo Solórzano" occupies pages 200–28.

I. Articles

GARCÍA GÓMEZ, EMILIO. "Boccaccio y Castillo Solórzano," *Revista de filología española*, 15 (1928), 376–78. Points out the origin of an episode in *The She-Stoat*. It concerns the dress "borrowed" and returned in the duped husband's presence, and at his insistence (*Decameron*, 8, 2).

LA GRONE, GREGORY G. "Castillo Solórzano's *Escarmientos de amor moralizados*," *Hispania*, 22 (1939), 61–67. Disposes of an awkward bibliographical item (*Varios y honestos entretenimientos*. México: 1625), by showing it has no connection with Castillo. Revisions of *Warnings of Love Moralized* as Castillo transposed it into *Lisardo in Love* are shown to be in the interests of clarity.

SIMON DÍAZ, JOSÉ. "Textos dispersos de clásicos españoles. III Castillo Solórzano," *Rivista de literatura*, 16 (1959), 31–32; 165–69. Some routinely phrased sonnets and *décimas* by Castillo have been gleaned from the preliminary pages of several little known books.

KENNEDY, RUTH LEE. "Pantaleón de Ribera, 'Sirene', Castillo y Solórzano [*sic*] and the Academia de Madrid in Early 1625." *Homage to John M.Hill. In Memoriam*, edited by Walter Poesse. Madrid and Bloomington, Indiana: Castalia, 1968, pp. 189–200. Among the three poems in the *Segunda Parte* of the works of Tirso de Molina (Madrid: 1635) is a "Reply" ("Respuesta") by Castillo to his friend Anastasio Pantaleón's letter concerning the latter's misadventures, in the spring of 1625 with a courtesan called Sirene. The literary society background is well illuminated.

BERNADACH, MOÏSE. "Castillo Solórzano et ses fantaisies parodiques (à propos d'une ingénieuse utilisation des romances)," *Revue des langues romanes*, 80 (1973), 149–75. Notes that Castillo left 21,509 lines of verse! Points out Castillo's versatility in devising unusual rhymes and, in the case of his "A la fuerza de Lucrecia," in splicing the old ballads of Spain into the "burlesque epyllion." Bernadach offers his translation into French.

Index

LIBRARY OF DAVIDSON COLLEGE

Books on regular loan may be checked out for **two weeks**. Books must be presented at the Circulation Desk in order to be renewed.

A fine is charged after date due.

Special books are subject to special regulations at the discretion of the library staff.